DEATH
INVESTIGATION
Systems and Procedures

DEATH INVESTIGATION
Systems and Procedures

Randy Hanzlick

CRC Press
Taylor & Francis Group
Boca Raton   London   New York

CRC Press is an imprint of the
Taylor & Francis Group, an informa business

CRC Press
Taylor & Francis Group
6000 Broken Sound Parkway NW, Suite 300
Boca Raton, FL 33487-2742

International Standard Book Number-10: 1-4200-4475-3 (Softcover)
International Standard Book Number-13: 978-1-4200-4475-1 (Softcover)

Library of Congress Cataloging-in-Publication Data

Hanzlick, Randy.
    Death investigation : systems and procedures / Randy Hanzlick.
        p. ; cm.
    Includes bibliographical references and index.
    ISBN-13: 978-1-4200-4475-1 (alk. paper)
    ISBN-10: 1-4200-4475-3 (alk. paper)
    1. Forensic pathology. 2. Death--Causes--Classification. 3. Criminal investigation.
I. Title.
    [DNLM: 1. Coroners and Medical Examiners--organization &
administration--United States. 2. Documentation--methods--United States. 3.
Forensic Medicine--methods--United States. 4. Forensic Medicine--organization &
administration--United States.   W 800 H252d 2007]

    RA1063.4.H362 2007
    614'.1--dc22   2006021259

Visit the Taylor & Francis Web site at
http://www.taylorandfrancis.com

and the CRC Press Web site at
http://www.crcpress.com

Dedication

This book is dedicated to the National Association of Medical Examiners, an organization which I love, and to my wonderful wife, Mary McFall Hanzlick, PhD, whom I love even more. Mary has listened to me talk about death investigation for 25 years, has been kind enough to put up with such ramblings, and has worked and raised our children Caitlin and Marinna during those years. She spent tedious hours proofreading and finding hundreds of typos, poor word choices, and other grammatical and format errors in the first draft of this book. Any remaining errors are the sole responsibility of the author.

Randy Hanzlick, MD

Preface

Death Investigation: Systems and Procedures is the first book dedicated to the topic of death investigation from the standpoint of the laws and administrative and operational procedures that pertain to medical examiner and coroner systems in the United States. These systems are charged by law with the investigation of sudden and unexplained deaths, as well as those involving violence, injury, poisoning, and other selected circumstances.

This book does *not* describe how an investigator should conduct death investigations, and it is *not* a book about specific autopsy procedures or pathology. It does not teach one how to solve crimes. Rather, it contains concepts and principles about the death investigation systems established by governments, and provides information useful in better understanding what to expect if you, a family member, or a friend become involved in a death investigation because of a specific death that occurred. *Death Investigation: Systems and Procedures* was written as a resource for students, the public, and practicing death investigation professionals who have, in the past, found it difficult to find death investigation system information in a single reference source.

Death Investigation: Systems and Procedures begins with coverage of the basic types of death investigation along with the statutory basis for death investigation systems. Specific details are then provided about coroners, medical examiners, and other forensic scientists and personnel who may officially be part of a death investigation. The overall goals of death investigation are presented along with examples of each type of death investigation. The types of death investigation are described along with a brief summary of the specific type of system existing in each state. Special circumstances, such as mass fatality incidents, are briefly described. The last portion of the book covers some of the more practical considerations, such as the content of an autopsy report, the death certificate, what information you might expect when you request copies of death investigation documents, principles and issues related to evidence and expert witnesses, and a description of what a typical day may be like at a medical examiner's or coroner's office. A number of useful illustrations are included to facilitate understanding of the written text and provide a method of quick review.

Death Investigation: Systems and Procedures may be most useful to students who are preparing to become forensic scientists, pathologists, medical examiners, coroners, death investigators, crime scene technicians, or epidemiologists who will be working with data derived from death investigation systems. The general public should derive useful information as well, and professionals already practicing in the field of death investigation may also find this book useful for expanding their knowledge or teaching their classes. Law students and lawyers may also find information that will be useful in their practice as a result of having a better understanding of death investigation systems.

This book should be easy to read and understand for anyone who is a senior in high school or older. *Death Investigation: Systems and Procedures* could be a useful textbook in introductory courses relating to death investigation. It provides a common ground of understanding and suggests areas into which one may dig further if interested. For those interested, useful web sites and additional reading materials are provided at the end of the book.

Author

Randy Hanzlick, MD, is a board-certified forensic pathologist, professor of forensic pathology at Emory University School of Medicine, and chief medical examiner for Fulton County, Georgia. Born in Salem, Ohio, he graduated from college and medical school at The Ohio State University, where he also did his pathology training. After completing his forensic pathology training in Atlanta, Georgia, he remained in Atlanta and has worked in the field of death investigation since the early 1980s. He is a past president of the National Association of Medical Examiners and a former pathology/biology section officer for the American Academy of Forensic Sciences.

Dr. Hanzlick is active on numerous committees for professional organizations and on multiple federal panels and projects related to death investigation and death certification, such as the CDC Guidelines for Investigation of Sudden, Unexplained Infant Death and the National Institute of Justice Guide for Death Scene Investigators.

Author of a text, several manuals, and more than 150 journal publications, Dr. Hanzlick's major interest areas include the development of professional guidelines, improvement in death investigation practices, death certification and mortality data, electronic data system development and data sharing, and the role of the medical examiner in public health surveillance and epidemiological research. He has received multiple awards including the National Association of Medical Examiners' Outstanding Service Award for significant contributions to medicolegal death investigation in the United States, the American Academy of Forensic Sciences Pathology/Biology Section's Milton Helpern Award for outstanding contributions to forensic pathology, and the National Center for Health Statistics' (NCHS) Director's Award for outstanding contributions to the field of health statistics and the mission of the NCHS.

TABLE OF CONTENTS

PART I *General Aspects of Death Investigation 1*

Chapter 1 Why Know about Death Investigation?..3

Chapter 2 What Is a Death Investigation?..7
  Initial Collection of Information...7
  Scene Investigation 7
  Examination of the Body..7
  Ancillary Investigations 8
  Report Preparation 9
  Conclusion...10

Chapter 3 Basic Types of Death Investigation 11
  Medicolegal Death Investigation 11
  Institution-Based Death Investigation..11
  Private Death Investigation 12

Chapter 4 Public Health Death Investigations..13

Chapter 5 Who Actually Performs Death Investigations? 17

Chapter 6 The State and Local Nature of Medicolegal Death Investigation 21

Chapter 7 Where Are Death Investigations Conducted?...................................25

Chapter 8 How Death Investigations Are Funded...29

PART II *More on the People Who Investigate....... 31*

Chapter 9 Forensic Pathologists 33

Chapter 10 Coroners 35

Chapter 11 Medical Examiners 41

Chapter 12 Death Investigators..45

Chapter 13 Who Controls the Scene of Death?..47

Chapter 14 Forensic Scientists..49

PART III   Goals of Death Investigations 55

Chapter 15 Basic Goals of Medicolegal Death Investigation............................57

Chapter 16 Goals of Institution-Based and Private Death Investigations............59

PART IV   Examples of Death Investigations by Type... 61

Chapter 17 A Typical Institution-Based Death Investigation 63

Chapter 18 A Typical Private Death Investigation...69

Chapter 19 A Typical Medicolegal Death Investigation 73

Chapter 20 Death Investigation: The Rake Analogy..79

PART V   Specific Features of Medicolegal Death Investigations... 83

Chapter 21 What Types of Deaths Are Reportable to the Medical Examiner or Coroner? 85

Chapter 22 Examples of Medicolegal Death Investigation Systems 87

Chapter 23 Types of Medicolegal Death Investigation by State..........................89

PART VI   Special Circumstances............................. 99

Chapter 24 What about Mass Fatality Incidents?.............................. 101

Chapter 25 Deaths on Indian Reservations or Federal Property 103

PART VII   Other Death Investigation Topics......... 105

Chapter 26 Who May Give Permission for an Autopsy?.................................. 107

Chapter 27 The Autopsy Report... 109

Chapter 28 The Death Certificate 113

Chapter 29 Exhumations.. 119

Chapter 30 Death Investigation and Funeral Arrangements 121

Chapter 31 Principles of Evidence 123

Chapter 32 What Is an Expert? 127

Chapter 33 What If You Disagree?.. 129

Chapter 34 Death Investigation and Insurance Policies.................................. 131

Chapter 35 Classic Dilemmas in Death Investigation...................................... 133

Chapter 36 Professional Death Investigation Organizations............................ 137

Chapter 37 Access to Death Investigation Information 141

Chapter 38 Pronouncement of Death 143

Chapter 39 Deaths in Custody and Public Institutions..................................... 145

Chapter 40 Criminal and Civil Law Issues 147

Chapter 41 Sample Autopsy Report 149

    Reason for Performing an Examination 149
    Date and Time of Examination.. 149
    Postmortem x-rays 149
    Presentation, Clothing, and Personal Effects 149
    Features of Identification 150
    Diagnostic and Therapeutic Artifacts 150
    Postmortem Changes... 150
    External Examination... 150
    Internal Examination... 151
        Chest and Abdomen.. 151
            Cardiovascular System 151
            Respiratory System... 151
            Gastrointestinal System 151
            Hepatobiliary System 152
            Urogenital System 152
            Reticuloendothelial System 152
            Musculoskeletal System 152
            Endocrine System 152
        Neck 152
        Head 152
    Report of Histologic Sections... 153
    Other Procedures... 153
    Final Assessment... 153
        Clinical Information.. 153
        Autopsy Findings.. 154
    Summary and Comments... 154

Chapter 42 A Day at the Medical Examiner's Office....................... 157

Further Reading 161

Useful Web Sites 163

Index 165

Part I

General Aspects of Death Investigation

1 Why Know about Death Investigation?

You may ask why we need to learn about death investigation. What does it matter once a person is dead? There are several reasons why everyone should be familiar with death investigation:

1. *Legal.* A death may result from someone breaking the law, such as occurs when a murder takes place. Death investigation can provide information to help identify who may have committed the murder, as well as where, when, why, and how it occurred. Or, a death may result from some action or neglect that may not be a crime, but for which someone may be held responsible because of civil law, such as someone who dies because of an unsafe working environment. The information developed during the death investigation may be very important for use in court to inform the jury or court (judge) about what may have happened and to assist the jury in its deliberations.
2. *Public health and safety.* Some deaths may result from conditions that may pose a danger to the public, such as unusual contagious infections or deaths from environmental hazards such as carbon monoxide. Investigation of such deaths may provide information that can be used immediately to address public concerns and to help develop prevention strategies and programs for the future.
3. *Institutional concerns.* Deaths may occur in hospitals, nursing homes, mental institutions, prisons, and other institutions where there may be complaints that the institution's personnel made a mistake, were abusive, or were negligent. Death investigation can provide the institution and public with information that may be used to address such concerns.
4. *Medical care quality.* Medicine is not an exact science and the accuracy of diagnoses and effectiveness of some treatments are not always known prior to death. Death investigation provides information that may be used to evaluate diagnosis and treatment to bring about gradual, long-term improvements in the quality of medical care.
5. *Personal reasons.* You may someday be directly affected by a death and its investigation. The outcome of a death investigation might determine whether you inherit money, or whether you may have to pay money to someone because you were somehow responsible for a death. Or, perhaps, whether you might lose your freedom and face time in prison for an illegal act you committed (or were thought to have committed!) may depend on the facts developed during a death investigation. You might benefit by

Overall Role of Medical Examiners and Coroners

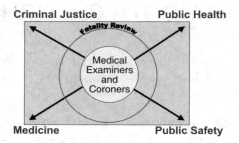

FIGURE 1.1   Medical examiners and coroners (MECs) have traditionally served the criminal justice system by investigating deaths that are due to violence, such as shootings and other forms of homicide, and providing reports that can be used when testifying in court when cases come to trial. MECs are also often called to testify in civil trials in cases of wrongful death, alleged malpractice, or product liability cases in which death may have been related to a defective or misused product. Autopsy findings are often used at medical conferences, such as those conducted by surgeons to review cases in which the patient died during or after surgery, in order to better understand surgical complications and to determine the extent of injuries and whether diagnosis and treatment were appropriate for the case. In recent years, MECs have also become important to public health and safety agencies who engage in programs to prevent illness and injury. For example, investigating several pedestrian deaths on one stretch of roadway may lead to the discovery that additional street lighting is needed in the area. It was investigation by medical examiners that led to the discovery of hantavirus pulmonary syndrome caused by rodents that spread disease. MECs also work closely with fatality review groups, such as the child fatality review panels that exist in virtually all states to review deaths of children to develop prevention strategies and correct agency-related problems in their work with families and children.

finding out from a death investigation that a family member has a genetic or other inherited disease that runs in your family, with which you might become afflicted, or for which tests or treatment might prolong your life or the life of a loved one such as your child. The quality and accuracy of death investigation should, therefore, be of direct interest and importance to you.

6. *Research*. Death investigation can provide information for use in research projects such as evaluating whether a new drug on the market is causing unexpected side effects or whether a new treatment actually does any good.

7. *Evaluation of transplant donors*. When a living person receives transplanted tissues or organs from a person who has died, death investigation of the donor can help determine whether the tissues or organs are healthy and free of disease that could adversely affect the recipient at some time in the future.

8. *You pay for death investigation*. If you are a taxpayer, some of the money you pay in taxes is used to pay for death investigations through the funding

of salaries, supplies, equipment, and buildings used in death investigation. You should be interested in the quality of death investigation to make sure you are getting what you pay for.

At some time in your life, you will undoubtedly face a situation where at least one of these aspects of death investigation impacts your life. It will be advantageous for you to have an understanding of death investigation so you are prepared when it happens.

2 What Is a Death Investigation?

When a death investigation occurs, there is a person who is primarily responsible for conducting the investigation. Who this person is depends on the circumstances. For deaths that do not involve injuries and that occur in hospitals, the person is usually a doctor (physician) called a *pathologist* who works at the hospital. For deaths that occur outside of a hospital or that involve an injury or are unexplained, the responsible person usually has the title of *medical examiner* or *coroner* and works for the local, county, or state government, and may or may not be a physician. These various types of people will be discussed in later chapters. Regardless of which type of person is responsible for the death investigation, there are certain steps that are usually followed or considered during the investigation (Figure 2.1).

INITIAL COLLECTION OF INFORMATION

This phase is usually the first phase of a death investigation and consists of collecting information about what is reported to have occurred prior to or near the time of death. This usually involves the collection of information about the decedent's medical and social history, activities before death, occupational history, and the circumstances leading up to death. It may be necessary to speak with numerous witnesses who knew the decedent or who may have witnessed some of the events leading to death.

SCENE INVESTIGATION

This aspect of death investigation involves going to the scene where death occurred, or perhaps to an area where the events leading to death occurred, if not both. During a scene investigation it may be necessary to take measurements, photographs, or to prepare videotapes or diagrams to adequately document the facts of the scene. Quite often, scene investigations are performed by the police or by a person who is acting on behalf of a medical examiner, coroner, or other person investigating the death. *Scene investigation* in the true sense is not usually done for deaths that occur in the hospital and which will not be investigated by a medical examiner or coroner.

EXAMINATION OF THE BODY

Death investigation often, but not always, involves examination of the body. This examination may be limited to examining only the outer aspect of the body (external

Death Investigation

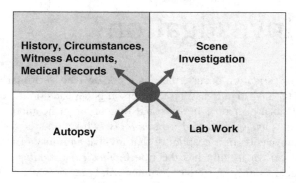

Must have them all!

FIGURE 2.1 Death investigation requires much more than just doing an autopsy. In many cases, the death scene investigation may be as or more important than the autopsy itself because the scene may provide valuable clues about the cause and circumstances of death. It is also quite common for the death investigation to include review of the decedent's medical records or other documents such as police reports and witness statements. In most cases it is also necessary to perform laboratory tests to analyze for disease or the presence of drugs. The need to perform all of these tasks may mean that a death investigation may take weeks or even months to be completed.

examination). Alternatively, a full autopsy, or perhaps a limited (restricted) autopsy may be performed in which only selected tissues or organs are examined. In some death investigations, if circumstances are well documented, it may not actually be necessary to examine the body. Usually the examination of the body is performed in a morgue or autopsy suite. However, the examination of the body may take place at the scene of the death or other place where the body is located at the time the investigation begins. If the examination is not done in a morgue, it is usually limited to an external examination of the body. On occasion, if there are no morgues available in the area, examination of the body may take place at a funeral home where autopsies are also sometimes performed. The equipment at funeral homes is quite similar to that in autopsy rooms.

The word *autopsy* is derived from Greek and means "a seeing for one's self," or a "seeing with one's own eyes." The word is usually used to describe procedures that involve opening of the body and examination of the various internal organs and tissues.

ANCILLARY INVESTIGATIONS

Many times it is necessary to perform tests or studies that lay outside the domain of the autopsy itself. Tests for the presence of drugs, for example, is one such investigation. As another example, it may be necessary for a firearms expert to examine a bullet or a gun to determine whether the bullet matches a suspected weapon or to evaluate whether or not a gun functions properly. Ancillary procedures may also involve the collection of reports from other agencies such as the person's doctor, the police, family and children services agencies, or other agencies that may have information relevant to the death.

REPORT PREPARATION

During the different phases of a death investigation, various reports are initiated and prepared, and then final reports are assembled in a *case record*. Usually, there is some sort of written report that summarizes the investigation, another report that details the findings when the body is examined (such as an autopsy report), and other reports that summarize the results of ancillary procedures, analyses, and tests. It is not unusual for a death certificate to be completed as well detailing the cause and manner of death, as well as other information about the decedent.

If you ever have a need to request reports for a death investigation, it is important for you to ask that *all* documents in a death investigation file be made available to you. If you simply ask for an autopsy report, that may be all that you receive, even if other types of records exist. It may be necessary for you to obtain reports from different sources because many agencies will only release documents that they originated; that is, they will not give you copies of documents they obtained from other agencies. In such cases, you may have to go back to the original source to get copies of some documents. Collecting such information can be somewhat time consuming because of the multiple agencies involved, but the extra work is often worth the time spent in tracking down the information.

It may be important or necessary for you to discuss the findings in a death investigation with the person who conducted the death investigation. In such cases you should contact that person and set up an appointment for a personal visit or telephone conversation, and talk to him or her personally about the findings. You should be sure to determine in advance the questions you want to ask and you should also be aware that some questions may be asked of you during such interviews or conversations.

Also realize that *final* reports may not truly be final. Most reports and opinions can be changed if information becomes available to warrant a change.

When death occurs in a hospital and the death investigation is conducted at the hospital by a hospital pathologist, the findings are usually given to the patient's doctor, who then discusses the findings with the patient's family. Any family member entitled to a copy of the medical records should also be entitled to receive a copy of the autopsy report. It is acceptable, however, for family members to contact the pathologist to discuss the findings directly. Also, when death investigation is conducted in the hospital by the hospital pathologist, a scene investigation is not usually required or performed, although examination of the area (scene) where death occurred may be necessary in some cases.

CONCLUSION

A typical death investigation includes an initial information collection phase, scene investigation, examination of the body, ancillary investigations and information collection, and report and case record preparation. Such case records are filed in some form so information from them may be retrieved when needed.

3 Basic Types of Death Investigation

There are three *basic types* of death investigations.

MEDICOLEGAL DEATH INVESTIGATION

Medicolegal death investigations are done because they are required or provided for by law. In certain types of death, usually those involving injury or those that are sudden and unexplained, the law provides a mechanism for death investigation to occur. Deaths due to homicide, suicide, accidents, and unexplained causes are common examples. Such investigations are usually performed by the local, county, or state governments, which have death investigation systems established for such purposes. Medicolegal death investigations are usually conducted by medical examiners and coroners, who will be more fully discussed in other chapters. Family permission is not usually required for medicolegal death investigations to occur because such investigations are required by law to enable collection of evidence and facts to resolve criminal or other legal issues that may arise because of the death. In some instances, the law may provide an opportunity for the family to object to a medicolegal death investigation or autopsy, but usually there is a mechanism for the medical examiner or coroner to conduct the examination or death investigation, if needed, despite a family's objections. In such cases, a court order may be needed to conduct the death investigation, but such cases are rare.

INSTITUTION-BASED DEATH INVESTIGATION

Institution-based death investigation is performed by or for institutions such as hospitals, nursing homes, or other medical facilities in which a patient may die. Institution-based death investigations usually require permission from the legal next of kin such as a spouse, sibling, parent, child, or other person who takes custody of the body for burial. Most institutions, such as hospitals, have a morgue (or have access to a morgue) and the death investigation is actually conducted within the institution or by some other agency that is affiliated with the institution acting on its behalf. Institution-based death investigation is usually done to answer certain questions related to the extent of disease or to evaluate the effectiveness of a diagnostic or therapeutic procedure, although there are other reasons that will be more fully discussed in other chapters.

PRIVATE DEATH INVESTIGATION

On occasion, a family member or legal next of kin may be interested in conducting their own death investigation outside of the medicolegal death investigation or institution-based death investigation options. In such cases the family may hire an attorney, a private investigator, a pathologist, or other person to perform (or arrange for) a death investigation, which may include autopsy. As an example, an individual may die in a hospital, but the family may have suspicions that the person was not treated appropriately. For whatever reasons, they may not trust the hospital to perform an autopsy as they may feel that the hospital may not be truthful or may try to hide something. The circumstances of the death may not qualify it for medicolegal death investigation. As a result, the only option may be for the family to arrange for their own death investigation in an attempt to answer questions that have arisen. In general, the autopsy portion of a private death investigation must be performed by a physician (usually a pathologist trained in such procedures).

In private death investigations, the family usually must bear the cost of the death investigation. Most often, the cost of a hospital or institution-based death investigation is born by the institution. There is usually no specific charge to the family for performance of autopsies in such cases, although there are some exceptions, especially if the family desires an autopsy but the hospital or institution does not feel that one is necessary. Medicolegal death investigations are also usually performed at the expense of the local, county, or state government that performs the investigation. The family is not usually billed for such investigations.

Death investigations (including autopsies) are sometimes performed as part of research protocols as well. For example, a hospitalized patient may have been on a treatment protocol in which a new experimental drug was being tested. The protocol has specific rules that must be followed in order to scientifically assess that new medication. Part of a protocol for patients who die may involve an autopsy to look for unexpected side effects or complications of the medication, or to evaluate its effectiveness. Although such death investigations may be done for research purposes, these usually qualify as institution-based autopsies because most clinical medical research projects are done in medical institutions. Thus, there is usually no charge to the family.

On occasion, a deceased person who had been a patient at an institution dies but is not a patient at the time of death. In some such instances, if the family wants the institution to perform an autopsy, the family may be billed for the service, although some places will not charge if the patient has an active medical record at the institution or the institution feels there is value in performing an autopsy.

4 Public Health Death Investigations

There is a fourth type of death investigation that differs somewhat from the three basic types described in the Chapter 3 (Figure 4.1). Public health death investigations are performed by public health agencies, such as local or state health departments, researchers, and federal agencies such as the Centers for Disease Control and Prevention (CDC). Generally, public health death investigations involve *retrospective* (afterward) study of groups (a *series*) of deaths to analyze the characteristics of the deaths with the goal of planning prevention, intervention, or response programs. The other forms of death investigation involve investigation of individual deaths *as they occur* to answer questions that have arisen about the specific death in question.

Two aspects of public health death investigation are *surveillance* and *epidemiologic research*. Surveillance has to do with monitoring the occurrence of certain types of death, such as identifying when and where they are occurring. Epidemiologic research has to do with analyzing the data from a group of similar deaths in an attempt to quantify the *incidence* (the number of new cases occurring) and *prevalence* (the number of cases that exist at any given time), and to identify possible causes and risk factors that place people at risk (*risk factors*) for the particular type of death. Thus, surveillance and epidemiologic research are aimed at prevention, control, and monitoring of a problem over time. For example, surveillance techniques detected the fact that there were excessive numbers of Native Americans dying in the southwestern U.S. a few years ago. Epidemiologists studied the deaths by reviewing medical records, conducting in-depth analyses of the lifestyles of the people involved as well as their habitats, and discovered that the problem was due to a virus (hantavirus) that was carried by rodents in areas with sanitation problems. This lead to elucidation of a new disease (hantavirus pulmonary syndrome) as well as the development of prevention and control measures. Because the cause of the illness was discovered and the typical features of the disease were clarified, greater awareness of the disease and improvement in diagnostic and treatment measures occurred. Thus, analysis of the dead ultimately benefited the living. There are numerous examples of how surveillance and epidemiologic research have identified and helped to control diseases, injuries, and other problems that may lead to human morbidity (illness) and mortality (death) (Figure 4.2).

Public health death investigations are funded, in general, by government dollars or by research grants from public and private institutions. In some cases, there may not be funding of specific public health death investigations. Rather, an agency is simply funded to study potential problems on a ongoing basis (such as the Agency for Toxic Substance and Disease Registry, at Centers for Disease Control and

Medicolegal	•Done under provision of state law •Paid for by taxes •Performed by medical examiner or coroner •Family permission not needed •Done in the public interest
Institution-Based	•Typically done at a hospital •Family permission is required •Paid for by the hospital or family •For research or evaluation of disease or medical care
Private	•Arranged and paid for by a family member or representative •A pathologist is paid for doing the autopsy •To address issues important to the family
Public Health	•For surveillance or retrospective epidemiological research related to conditions of public health importance •Often includes review of multiple deaths

FIGURE 4.1 Death investigations may be categorized into four major types based on the place, time, and purpose of the investigation. The characteristics of each can be summarized as shown above.

Drug Abuse Warning Network	Collects information about deaths caused by various types of drugs. See http://dawninfo.samhsa.gov
FDA MedWatch	Collects information about deaths involving medical products and devices. See http://www.fda.gov/medwatch
MECAP	Medical Examiner/Coroner Alert Program for deaths involving certain consumer products. See https://www.cpsc/gov/mecap.html
CDC	The Centers for Disease Control and Prevention has published numerous articles based on medical examiner and coroner data.
Others	National Institute of Occupational Safety and Health (NIOSH); Bureau of Labor Statistics (BLS); National Highway Traffic Safety Administration (NHTSA); National Institute of Justice (NIJ)

FIGURE 4.2 Federal agencies routinely rely upon medical examiner or coroner data.

Prevention). Other projects may be specifically funded to study a particular problem for a specified period of time.

It is not uncommon for teams of people to be sent into the field to conduct public health death investigations. They may actually move for a period of time and spend weeks or months in a given location to conduct their investigations. For example, several years ago in California there was a reported increase in the number of infant deaths resulting from an infection (epiglottitis) that causes the airways to close off, suggesting a possible emerging public health problem. For several months, epidemiologists studied the problem by going to the area involved, reviewing records, talking with families, reviewing the autopsy findings, and collecting background information on the babies who died and their families. When the investigation was complete, it was concluded that there was probably not a significant health problem. This investigation allayed fears of an epidemic and resulted in suggestions for improving the diagnosis of epiglottitis to avoid such problems in the future. Conducting such investigations costs money, but the expense is usually justified because the investigation will show that there is either nothing to worry about or that a real problem exists that can be addressed to ensure public health or safety.

Public health death investigations are frequently conducted in cooperation with the medical examiner or coroner through review of their records and investigative findings. Remember, it is the medical examiner or coroner who often investigates deaths that are unexpected and are of public health interest, and the medical examiner's or coroner's information is needed to make the public health death investigation complete.

The other parts of this book deal only with the three basic types of death investigation — medicolegal, institution-based, and private. This brief discussion of public health death investigation was included for completeness and to show how death investigation might be conducted on a scale and for a purpose that goes beyond an individual death investigation.

Because of the important relationships among medical examiners, coroners, and the public health, in 1985 the Centers for Disease Control and Prevention (CDC) established a Medical Examiner/Coroner Information Sharing Program to facilitate relationships and exchange of information between the death investigation and public health communities.

5 Who Actually Performs Death Investigations?

The person responsible for conducting a death investigation depends on the type of investigation. Medicolegal death investigations are usually performed by medical examiners, coroners, or similar officials acting on behalf of the government. Institution-based death investigations are usually conducted by pathologists who work at or for the institution. Although private death investigations may employ private investigators or detectives, the medical portion is usually performed by a pathologist or other physician with training in autopsy and death investigation. Although there may be differences in the meanings of the words *medical examiner, coroner,* and *pathologist,* such titles may involve qualifications that overlap somewhat. Specific descriptions of these various types of people will now be offered to facilitate understanding.

A *pathologist* is a physician who has had special training in the field of pathology. The word *pathology* literally means the "study of suffering." Usually, of course, suffering is due to disease or injury. To become a pathologist, one must go to medical school and become a medical doctor, or as an alternative, go to an osteopathic school of medicine and become a doctor of osteopathy. After graduating from medical school, such physicians may enroll in basic training in the field of pathology. The specialty of pathology provides training in the study of tissues, organs, and systems in terms of how disease processes are manifested through symptoms, signs, visible changes in organs and tissues, and functional abnormalities that can be measured with laboratory tests. Pathologists also study how diseases come about and evolve (*pathogenesis*). Much of the training for pathologists includes examination of specimens removed at surgery (such as a gallbladder or appendix that has been taken out during a surgical procedure) or through the performance of autopsies in which the various organs and tissues of the body are examined, referred to as *anatomic pathology.* Such examination includes looking at the tissue with the naked eye, examining it under the microscope, and subjecting body fluids and tissues to a number of tests in the laboratory. The performance of laboratory tests also falls into the field of pathology, and is referred to as *clinical pathology.* Training in pathology after medical school requires somewhere between 3 and 5 years, depending on the type of training that is desired, and whether training is taken in anatomic pathology, clinical pathology, or both.

After basic pathology training, some pathologists can do specialized training for a year or more in the area of *forensic pathology,* in which specific training in death investigation is offered. *Forensic* means "open to public discussion and debate," or "belonging to the courts." Thus *forensic pathology* is a subspecialty of pathology that deals with pathology and its relevance to public and court or legal issues. This type of training usually consists of spending a year at an approved (accredited) medical examiner's or coroner's office observing and participating in death investigations that are of the medicolegal type.

The American Board of Pathology is a professional organization that offers an examination the pathologist may take to show that he or she has undergone a formal educational curriculum and has achieved a minimum level of competence in the field. Not all pathologists take or successfully pass the examination, but in some settings they may still practice if they have a medical license. Once the pathologist has completed the basic training, he or she can apply for the examination and if accepted, is considered to be *board qualified*. If the examination is then taken and successfully completed (i.e., the pathologist passes the examination), he or she is said to be *board certified*. There is a board examination for anatomic pathology and another for clinical pathology. There are also subspecialty examinations the pathologist may take in areas such as dermatopathology, neuropathology, and forensic pathology.

Most pathologists who conduct death investigations and perform autopsies are board qualified or board certified in anatomical pathology. This especially holds true for those who work in hospitals and conduct institution-based death investigations, because many institutions require that their doctors be board certified in the field of their medical practice. Pathologists who conduct medicolegal death investigations are often not only qualified in anatomic pathology (and perhaps clinical pathology), but in forensic pathology as well. In fact, many places that employ medical examiners require that the medical examiner be a board qualified or certified forensic pathologist, although this is not always the case.

It pays to be familiar with the type of training that a pathologist has had if that pathologist is involved in a death investigation. Not all pathologists have had exactly the same training, and of course not all of them are as good at death investigation as some others may be. Particularly when arranging for a private death investigation, it is prudent to determine whether or not the pathologist is board certified in forensic pathology. Board certification indicates that the pathologist has undertaken an established set of training materials and educational courses and has successfully completed an examination that is offered by professional peers to ensure that the person has attained a minimal level of competence in the field.

In summary, a pathologist is one who has completed medical or osteopathic school (i.e., is a physician), at least 3 and probably closer to 5 additional years training in anatomic and/or clinical pathology, and if a forensic pathologist, an additional year of special training of forensic pathology. Thus, the total training time required after graduation from college to become a forensic pathologist is a minimum of about 8 years. Most people who start college at age 18 will be 30 or 31 years old when all necessary training is completed.

Some medicolegal death investigations are conducted by *coroners*. The history of coroners is presented in Chapter 10. At this point, it needs to be noted that a coroner is usually an elected official who is charged with the responsibility of medicolegal death investigation, usually for a single county. Almost all coroners in the U.S. are elected at the county level, although in a few areas coroners are appointed, and they may serve regions larger than a single county. Not all states have coroners. Approximately 28 states have counties with coroners who conduct death investigations. Some states have coroners in every county, while other states may only have coroners in some counties while other counties or areas have other types of medicolegal death investigation systems that do not involve a coroner (see below). The requirements for being elected as coroner are often minimal, often requiring only that the person be eligible to run for public office. Only a few states require that the coroner be a physician (Louisiana, Ohio, North Dakota, and Kansas). When a coroner is required to be a physician, it is usually not required that the coroner be a pathologist. Thus, coroners consist of a wide variety of people whose job responsibilities and death investigation abilities vary substantially. Many coroners serve while they also carry out another full-time job or occupation. It is not uncommon for coroners to be in the funeral business, although many industries and trades are represented among coroners in the U.S., and in recent years, more and more coroners have backgrounds in medical or paramedical fields. In the U.S. there are 3137 counties. In the 28 states that have coroners, there are more than 2,000 different coroners.

Your first question will probably be: "If a coroner does not have to be a physician, how can he investigate deaths, and particularly, how can he or she perform autopsies?" The answer is that, usually, coroners have access to a physician or an anatomic or forensic pathologist who can perform autopsies for them. Such persons are often referred to as a *coroner's pathologist*. Thus, in most areas with coroners, there is a working relationship between the coroner and a physician, pathologist, or forensic pathologist who can assist in the performance of autopsies and death investigations. The coroner's main job is to collect the information about the death, to document the information, and to ensure that the death certificate is completed on appropriate deaths. In doing so, the coroner may rely heavily on others. In addition, coroners in many areas may hold what is referred to as an *inquest* in which a jury is assembled from members of the public to hear the facts of the death investigation and to make a decision about the circumstances of death. Most states do not require that the coroner hold an inquest, and the coroner often makes decisions about the circumstances of death based on the information he or she has collected. However, in cases that are difficult or in which there is public interest, the coroner may hold an inquest so that the public can be involved in a decision about the circumstances surrounding a death. Sometimes the law allows for or requires that an inquest be held in certain types of circumstances, such as deaths in prison. Also, the law or financial capabilities of the county may limit annual funds for inquests so that the potential number of annual inquests is limited. Inquests are held to involve the public as inquest jury members, although some claim that inquests may result in verdicts that are not accurate because jury members who are "average citizens" may not appreciate the scientific aspects of a given case. Thus, there are pros and cons when considering the merits of the coroner inquest system.

The title of *medical examiner* is confusing because it means different things in different states. In general, however, medical examiners are physicians who are appointed by state, county, or local governments to conduct or oversee medicolegal death investigations. Usually the governments require that the medical examiner be a physician, and many require that the medical examiner be a pathologist or a forensic pathologist.

Many counties have abolished the office of coroner and created in its place the office of medical examiner. This has usually been done in recognition of the fact that it is advantageous to have persons with medical knowledge and training be in charge of medicolegal death investigation. Thus, in the strictest sense of the title, the title of medical examiner applies to a physician (often a pathologist or forensic pathologist) who is appointed by the local or state government to perform medicolegal death investigations. Also in the strictest sense, the medical examiner title is used in areas where there is not a coroner because the office of coroner has been abolished. However, as previously discussed, the title of medical examiner is defined differently by different states. In North Carolina and Michigan, for example, a medical examiner may be a physician who assists in death investigations, but may not be directly responsible for performing an autopsy. Such people may go to the scene and examine bodies but may not perform autopsies. The only way to be sure what the title of *medical examiner* means is to determine how it is defined in state or local law. Throughout the remainder of this book, the title of medical examiner will be used to describe a person who is responsible for medicolegal death investigation in areas where there is no official with the title of coroner.

Medical examiners differ from coroners not only in their training, but also in the populations they serve. As previously mentioned, most coroners serve at the county level with few exceptions. Medical examiners, however, may serve at the city level, the county level, on the regional or multicounty level, and in approximately 21 states, at the statewide level. Many states (such as Maryland) have a statewide medical examiner system in which a single medical examiner oversees all medicolegal death investigations in the state, although death investigations may be conducted out of several regional or district offices located throughout the state. In some state systems, such as that in New Mexico, all death investigations are conducted in a single office. Again, practices and systems vary by state and will be discussed in greater detail in a later chapter.

In summary, an anatomic pathologist is a physician who has been trained in autopsy performance and pathology, and a forensic pathologist is an anatomic pathologist who has received additional specific training in medicolegal death investigation. Each may serve as a medical examiner or coroner, although some medical examiners may not be pathologists, and many coroners are not physicians. There are no clear cut, uniformly applicable definitions for medical examiners and coroners because definitions and duties vary by state. In general, anatomic pathologists conduct institution-based death investigations, while medical examiners and coroners conduct medicolegal death investigations. Private death investigations may be conducted by whoever the next of kin designates, but usually an anatomic or forensic pathologist will be involved if an autopsy is performed.

6 The State and Local Nature of Medicolegal Death Investigation

Although there are federal laws and rules that may govern the court system and evidence, there are no national death investigation laws. As a consequence, medicolegal death investigations are performed in each state under the specific laws of that state. Local (i.e., city or county) legal codes or laws may also modify these various state laws. As a consequence, the types of deaths that are investigated in each state may vary, although there are certain types of deaths that are fairly consistently investigated.

In 1954, a Model Postmortem Examinations Act was developed for states to use as a guide when developing their own laws. Unfortunately, most states either developed their own laws independently of the model law, or modified the model law to meet their own needs. The result is death investigation practices that vary from state to state.

The Centers for Disease Control and Prevention previously published a directory entitled *Death Investigation in the United States and Canada*. Much of the manual contents is now available on the CDC web site at www.cdc.gov/epo/dphsi/mecisp/index.htm, although some of the material is in need of updating. The CDC information has proven to be a valuable resource for persons who are studying death investigation, and familiarity with its contents is highly recommended. In this primer, we will not discuss the individual laws of each state because that topic would fill a whole book by itself. However, selected features of medicolegal death investigations in each state will be discussed in a later chapter.

Each state has a law that addresses death investigation of various types. These laws are usually referred to as *state autopsy laws* or *state death investigation laws*, *postmortem examination laws* (or acts), or *state anatomy laws*. The major portion of such laws usually addresses medicolegal death investigations. However, most states also have laws that briefly address the performance of death investigations and autopsies in other settings, such as hospitals. These laws regarding institution-based autopsies usually give the physicians or pathologists at a hospital or other institution the right to perform an autopsy if permission is obtained from the legal next of kin (family member), and usually specifies who those persons must be and their order of preference in giving consent for autopsy. Such laws also may address what must be done with organs or tissues that are removed from bodies.

It is important for you to remember that death investigation laws vary among the states. For example, some states (such as Delaware) require that deaths under

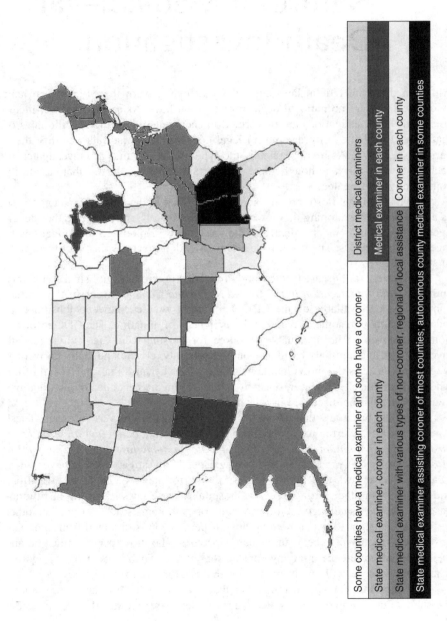

Some counties have a medical examiner and some have a coroner

District medical examiners

State medical examiner, coroner in each county

Medical examiner in each county

State medical examiner with various types of non-coroner, regional or local assistance

Coroner in each county

State medical examiner assisting coroner of most counties; autonomous county medical examiner in some counties anesthesia be investigated by the medical examiner, whereas some other states do not require such investigations. This means that on a national level, such deaths are inconsistently investigated. Persons who wish to study such deaths must determine where they are investigated routinely in order to know where to find appropriate information for their studies. It also means that you must know the laws of your state to know what types of death are investigated there. Remember that in a hospital, if a death were to occur under anesthesia and the state laws did not mandate investigation by the medical examiner or coroner, family permission would have to be given for an autopsy to be performed as an institution-based death investigation. If for some reason the permission of the next of kin could not be obtained, or if the family opted not to give permission, then an investigation would not occur unless the family arranged for a private death investigation. The hospital may review certain medical records, of course, and without the family's permission, but a critical portion of the investigation — the autopsy — could not be performed without family permission.

Thus, the types of death that are subject to medicolegal death investigation vary by state, and familiarity with specific provisions of state law is necessary (Figure 6.1).

FIGURE 6.1 (facing page) There is no federal death investigation system. Rather, each state has its own laws describing the death investigation system and which deaths are to be investigated. Nearly every state has something unique about its death investigation system, which makes classification with other states difficult. For example, state medical examiners exist in the states shown in gray or black above. However, Virginia has district offices that report to the state medical examiner; North Carolina might be best described as having county medical examiners with oversight by a state medical examiner; and Montana has a state medical examiner but also has a coroner in every county. Other states with state medical examiners also have unique features in the way they operate in conjunction with local assistants at the regional or county level. The map opposite is just one way to classify death investigation systems. See Chapter 23 for more details.

7 Where Are Death Investigations Conducted?

The venue for conducting a death investigation depends on the phase of the investigation. Of course, the scene investigation is typically conducted wherever the death occurs, where a dead body is found, or where the events leading to death are thought or known to have occurred. No matter what type of death investigation occurs, there is usually someone — a policeman, the local coroner, the medical examiner, or even a physician or pathologist in a hospital — who is available to inspect the scene if necessary. Most scene investigations occur in homes and residences or in businesses (places where people work), because that is where people who are not hospitalized tend to spend most of their time, and hence where they tend to die.

Where the autopsy or examination of the body occurs depends on the facilities available in the area. Most major metropolitan areas have a county morgue or similar facility (although many are relatively old and out of date), where autopsies and examinations may be performed. This, of course, often results in a body having to be transferred from where it was found or died to another location for examination.

In many jurisdictions, however, especially those that are low in population or are rural, there may be no specific morgue facility available for examination of the body. In such instances, it is not uncommon for the coroner to have arrangements with the nearest hospital that may allow the coroner to use the morgue facility in the hospital for examination when needed. In some instances, because there are almost always funeral homes within a short distance, some autopsies and bodily examinations are performed in funeral homes. The equipment used to prepare bodies for funeral and burial is quite similar to that used to perform an autopsy, and in many instances funeral homes are suitable places to perform postmortem examinations, although a specific morgue facility is more desirable.

In terms of the other aspects of the investigation, such as the processing of evidence, most states have at least one facility that is operated by the state police or similar agency and is often referred to as a *crime laboratory, police laboratory*, or *forensic science lab*. Here, the many different types of forensic scientists work and process their evidence in the laboratories provided in these facilities. In many areas, the evidence must be transported a long distance to be processed. For example, in Georgia, although there are several branch laboratories under the auspices of the state crime laboratory, the major laboratory is located in Atlanta and much of the evidence is often transferred across the state to Atlanta for processing. A similar situation exists in many other states.

FIGURE 7.1 Most cities or counties with large populations, many smaller counties, and some states have specific buildings that house the medical examiner's or coroner's office. Many facilities, such as the Fulton County Medical Examiner's Center (FCME) in Atlanta, are designed so that all investigative and autopsy procedures may be done at the facility. The FCME facility has three buildings including administration and offices (front building), an autopsy building (middle building with green awning), and a smaller building (left rear of photo) in which autopsies are conducted on bodies that are decomposed, skeletonized, or pose special risks to workers. Each building is separate from the others, has its own air supply, and is specially constructed to promote occupational safety and health. The main autopsy building has eight autopsy stations and the smaller building has two, allowing for multiple autopsies to be performed at the same time. In some locations the medical examiner's or coroner's department is its own office within county or state government, while in other locations the office may be part of a crime lab, police department, or health department. Some offices are affiliated with medical schools, but most are not.

In terms of housing for the medical examiner, coroner, or other person who conducts death investigations, many jurisdictions also have a specific physical plant or building designed especially for the medical examiner or coroner, particularly in metropolitan areas (Figure 7.1 and Figure 7.2). In many areas, however, the coroner or medical examiner may be provided only with a small office at the police department, at the court house, or in some other government complex. In still other areas, particularly rural areas, the coroner may operate and keep his records out of his home, his place of business, or some other location. Remember, many coroners and persons who investigate deaths do so on a part-time basis and have additional jobs, perhaps even full-time, in addition to being the coroner. Thus, in many areas, there may not be a specific coroner's office. It is not uncommon to look in various directories for a coroner's phone number, and upon calling the number, reach the coroner's residence or place of usual business.

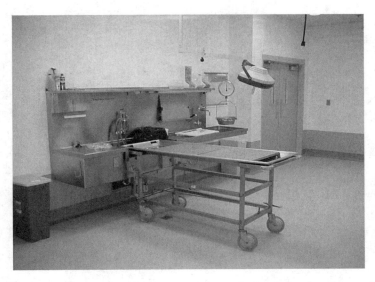

FIGURE 7.2 A typical autopsy work station at a medical examiner's or coroner's office. The body is placed on the cart when it arrives at the morgue and remains on the same cart during and after the autopsy until release to the funeral home. The work station has an area to examine organs, a scale to weigh organs, overhead lighting, and an overhead power supply for the vibrating (oscillating) saws that are used to cut bone. A writing board is also present so that notes may be taken. The containers on the top shelf (on right) contain the cassettes into which small samples of tissue are placed and kept in formalin until they are prepared for examination under the microscope. The large container on the floor (at left) is where used needles and scalpel blades are placed so workers are protected from cuts and punctures, and so they may be destroyed safely. The hose is used to provide water and for suction to remove blood and body fluids that are present in the body cavities at autopsy.

Thus, as with many other aspects of death investigation, the place in which the various components of medicolegal death investigation are conducted differ depending on location, and are based primarily on available resources, such as funding and physical facilities.

Institution-based death investigations are usually conducted in a morgue (autopsy room) in the institution. However, some institutions lack morgue facilities and may transport bodies to another facility for examination. Private death investigations are often conducted at the hospital where the pathologist who will perform the autopsy usually works, or in a local medical examiner's or coroner's morgue or funeral home, depending on availability and the ability to make suitable arrangements. Because morgues are few, most morgue facilities allow their space to be used or rented by persons conducting private death investigations.

In some instances, existing morgue facilities may be inadequate. For example, in a *mass disaster* such as a plane crash, where hundreds of people may be killed, *temporary morgue facilities* may be needed. In such instances, trucks, warehouses, or tents may be used and temporarily equipped with the necessary equipment to conduct the various components of death investigations including autopsies.

8 How Death Investigations Are Funded

The funding of private death investigations is a simple matter. Basically, whoever requested the investigation be performed is responsible for paying the bills. Usually this is a family member (next of kin) of the deceased.

In most instances, institution-based death investigations are also a simple matter in terms of funding. There are often no specific charges levied by the hospital or institution for the performance of an institution-based death investigation and autopsy. Institutions do receive federal dollars that are used to support the autopsy and death investigation service, and some funds from other billings are also used to support the autopsy service. Thus, the institution generates an overhead amount of money which is used to support the autopsy service. Usually the pathologists are on a salary and there is no specific billing on a case-by-case basis, and the institution often has a morgue with ongoing expenses for lighting, supplies, and so forth. Therefore, the financial impact on the hospital, whether the institution performs 50 autopsies a year or 75, is negligible because costs are relatively fixed. The morgue and the doctors are already there, and the autopsy cases and death investigations are conducted as needed. The cost for supplies to do an autopsy is relatively small, and most expenses involve the tissue processing and lab tests that may be done. However, in recent years with rising costs of health care and medical personnel, some institutions have begun to charge if an autopsy is performed. Be sure to find out if you will be billed for an autopsy performed in a hospital.

Medicolegal death investigation systems are usually funded by the local, county, or state government. This money, of course, comes from tax dollars. Most counties have some sort of formula they use based on the population of the county, and a certain dollar amount is allocated each year based on the population of the area (*per capita costs*). The nature of the deaths that occur in the area also play a role, as some areas have much higher death rates than others, and further, some areas have higher rates of violent deaths, such as homicides, suicides, and accidents, than others. Typically, these high death and violence rates are in metropolitan areas. Also, per capita income and taxation vary from place to place, and this also plays a role with respect to how much money is available for death investigation. The per capita dollar amount varies widely from place to place and is as low as 50 cents per capita per year in some areas and several dollars or more per capita in others. As you might imagine, the quality of the death investigation services depend considerably on the degree to which the death investigation offices are funded. Most experts consider $1.00 per capita per year as an absolute minimum level of funding to operate a death investigation system, with $2.00 per capita being a more reasonable minimum level.

Part II

More on the People Who Investigate

9 Forensic Pathologists

You might ask: "Why, if forensic pathologists are especially trained in autopsy and death investigation, do they not perform all medicolegal death investigations in the United States?" The answer is simple — there simply aren't enough of them, and there may never be.

It is estimated that it would take approximately 800 to 1000 full-time forensic pathologists to conduct and oversee all death investigations in the U.S. Unfortunately, since the first board examination in forensic pathology in 1960, there have been only about 1300 people certified in forensic pathology (Figure 9.1). During that time, many of those people have died, or retired. Further, not all people who are board certified in forensic pathology practice it full time or at all.

Another problem is that there are very few forensic pathology training programs. There are only about 40 places in the country in which one can train in forensic pathology, with a total of approximately 70 positions available per year. Unfortunately, some of those positions are either unfunded or unfilled each year, meaning that every year, there are only about 35 to 40 board certified forensic pathologists produced. This is not enough to keep up with death and other forms of attrition.

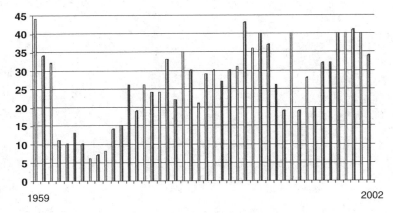

FIGURE 9.1 The American Board of Pathology first offered board certification in forensic pathology in 1959. Between 1959 and 2002, about 1,150 physicians became certified in forensic pathology, with approximately 30 to 40 new certifications per year. The number of board certified forensic pathologists is not enough to meet current needs or to keep up with attrition due to retirements, deaths, and those who leave the field. In comparison, about 5,000 physicians go into internal medicine training each year. (Data from the American Board of Pathology, Tampa, FL.)

To make matters worse, general training in pathology is a prerequisite to training in forensic pathology. Fewer people are entering this field now than in the past, which has to do with many factors including, but not limited to, trends toward managed care in medicine, and the fact that pathologists rank fairly low with respect to income level among physicians. Thus, if fewer people are going into pathology, there may be fewer people going into forensic pathology as a result.

In the past, the American Board of Pathology allowed pathologists who had two years of experience in forensic pathology, but who did not necessarily enroll in an approved training program, to sit for the board examination. Now, only those individuals who have trained in an approved forensic pathology training program are eligible to sit for the board examination. This may have the net effect of also reducing the number of board certified forensic pathologists. However, it will ensure that those individuals who are board certified have indeed gone through an approved training program.

Thus, there is a positive side and a negative side regarding the small number of forensic pathologists. On the positive side, the job market for forensic pathologists looks good because there aren't enough to go around. On the negative side, death investigation may suffer because the lack of fully trained and qualified individuals requires that persons who are less qualified and experienced conduct death investigations, compromising the quality of death investigations in some areas of the nation.

10 Coroners

Some people have complained about coroners and wonder why they are allowed to conduct death investigations when they have little or no training or experience in medicine or science (Figure 10.1). Part of the reason may have to do with the history of death investigation of which coroners were an early part, and part of it has to do with the supply of trained and qualified people. Coroners have been around since the year 1194 when the English *Articles of Eyre* were written, which required that three knights and a clerk attend each death (Figure 10.2). These persons were known as *custos placitorum coronae* — Keepers of the Pleas of the Crown. The Latin word for crown is *corona*, and the word *coroner* is derived from this term. A major task of the "coroners" back in the twelfth century was to ensure that the proper portion of a dead person's assets were secured for the crown. Thus, originally, coroners served somewhat of the same function as the Internal Revenue Service serves today. They also, however, made inquiries to determine the cause and circumstances of death and enforced the *lex murdrorum*, a law prohibiting homicide and the origin of today's word *murder* (Figure 10.3).

Through the years, the functions of coroners changed more toward actually investigating the cause and circumstances of death. When the English settlers came to North America in the 1600s, they brought the coroner system with them. Thus the early death investigation practices in this country were similar to those in England. Laws were gradually written that paralleled the English system, and thus coroners became an integral part of death investigation in the U.S. It was not until the mid to late 1800s in Massachusetts and Maryland that evolution began toward the medical investigation of death. There had been recognition in England of the need for medical knowledge in the investigation of deaths, and a coroners' act passed in the late 1800s required that a physician at least attend all deaths to ascertain medical information related to death investigation.

So it can be seen that coroners have been around for nearly a millennium. The persistence of coroners today has not only grown out of this history, but has also been necessitated by the lack of sufficient numbers of trained persons to conduct death investigation. There are simply not enough doctors trained in death investigation to conduct all death investigations in the U.S. Further, as you can imagine, physicians are much more expensive to hire than are laypersons who may be able to conduct death investigations as a part-time job. One must realize that in many areas, in a given year, there may only be a few deaths that require medicolegal investigation, and to hire a physician to investigate these may be prohibitively expensive. Physicians who are trained in death investigation may not be attracted to areas with such small case loads. All of these factors have led to the continuation of coroners in some areas.

To Serve as a Coroner in Georgia...

- Must be a registered voter
- Minimum age 25 years
- No felony convictions
- High school diploma or equivalent
- Must sign affidavit attesting to above
- Annual training required (1 week)

Requirements are similar in many states

FIGURE 10.1   In most states that have coroners, he or she is not required to be a physician and the requirements to hold office may be relatively simple, such as those shown for the state of Georgia. Because coroners are often not physicians, they must rely on physician pathologists to perform autopsies when needed. Such persons are usually referred to as *coroner's pathologists* or sometimes as *medical examiners*. When the term medical examiner is used, it is important to understand the local definition because definitions, job duties, and requirements vary among the states.

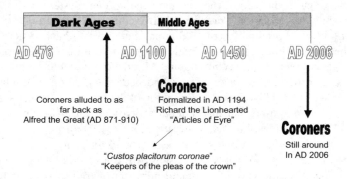

Coroner Time Line

Dark Ages	Middle Ages	

AD 476   AD 1100   AD 1450   AD 2006

Coroners
Coroners alluded to as far back as Alfred the Great (AD 871-910)
Formalized in AD 1194 Richard the Lionhearted "Articles of Eyre"

"Custos placitorum coronae" "Keepers of the pleas of the crown"

Coroners
Still around In AD 2006

FIGURE 10.2   Coroners date back to at least AD 1194 in England when the Articles of Eyre required that three knights and a clerk attend death scenes to determine what happened and to collect appropriate taxes for the crown. These persons were referred to as *custos placitorum coronae* (keepers of the pleas of the crown), which is where the word *coroner* is thought to have originated. When the colonists settled in America, they brought the English system of common law with them. In fact, the state of Georgia's first constitution of 1777 mentions coroners. Medical examiners did not emerge until the late 1800s.

Another aspect of coroners is their political nature. They are often people who are well known locally, which of course enables them to become elected. They often have strong political ties locally to persons who would have to change the laws to abolish the office of coroner, hence they tend to favor the current system and keep the coroner system intact.

Historical Duties of the Coroner

- Hold inquests
- Enforce the "Lex Murdrorum"
- Place a value on objects
- Get arrest warrants
- Confiscate property
- Investigate treasure troves

FIGURE 10.3 Centuries ago, coroners not only investigated deaths, but also served to ensure that appropriate property and assets were collected for the crown. Inquests were held to determine the circumstances surrounding death. The *lex murdrorum* was a law against murder, and coroners also investigated deaths to rule out murder. They could confiscate property (for taxes or as evidence) and get arrest warrants. Their tax-related duties included placing value on various objects and investigating treasure troves. Today, coroners still perform the duties related to death investigation, evidence, and inquests, but their collection of valuables and property is done mainly so that it is safeguarded for return to the rightful owner, or so that it may be used as evidence, if needed. (Information on coroners obtained from www.Brittania.com.)

Coroners have also been maligned because many are in the funeral business. People claim that they become the coroner so they can arrive at the scenes of sudden and unexpected deaths and recruit business for their funeral homes. This may or may not be true, but in some states there are specific laws that prohibit funeral directors from being coroners, or at least state that they may not engage in activities that constitute a potential conflict of interest. You can imagine the potential conflict if someone in your family died suddenly and unexpectedly, the coroner comes to the house to investigate the death, and you have not had adequate time to make proper funeral arrangements. If you find out that the coroner is a funeral director, you may be tempted to use that person's funeral home and the coroner thus may generate business through his or her duties as the coroner. This is the type of conflict that has been of concern, but which is probably more of a theoretical concern than a real one.

Another complaint about coroners is that they must be reelected every 2 or 4 years, depending on how elections run in the county or state where they are elected. This means that there could potentially be turnover in the office of coroner every time there is an election. Such a phenomenon would be an obstacle to the accumulation of long-term experience. There are many coroners who have been repeatedly reelected, have held the office for many years, and who gained tremendous experience after having served as the coroner for a long time. However, one could imagine that if the office of coroner changed every few years, a new person may come into office who may have no particular knowledge of death investigation. Nevertheless, the concern is legitimate; contrast this to a medical examiner system in which the medical examiner may be appointed for an unspecified term and may be removed from office only for due cause, such as mishandling of the office. The appointment nature of the medical examiner system tends to promote long-term experience, whereas theoretically at least, the coroner system may foster turnover in a public office, which hampers long-term death investigation experience.

Most coroners could not be accused of taking the job because of money. Many are paid only a small amount each time they investigate a death or are paid only a small annual stipend for their services. In most areas, a person could not get rich by being the coroner. Most of these people have a true interest and dedication to death investigation and run for office because they are interested in the topic of death investigation. As mentioned, many coroners are funeral directors, embalmers, or other persons such as emergency medical technicians who have experience in dealing with families and dealing with deceased patients. However, there are also a considerable number of coroners who are businessmen or engaged in other occupations that don't necessarily involve deceased individuals or their families.

Although there are 28 states that have coroners, only a few require some sort of formal training for the coroners once they are elected, and only 4 states require the coroner to be a physician (Ohio, Louisiana, North Dakota, and Kansas). Even in states that require training, the training may be minimal, amounting to only 20 to 40 hours of training per year, or perhaps only an initial training course with no requirements for subsequent updating (Figure 10.4).

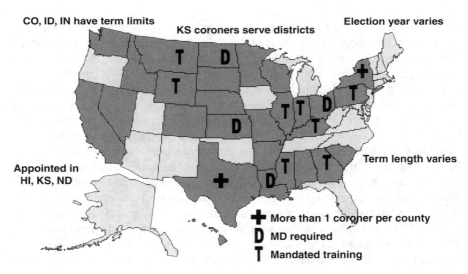

FIGURE 10.4 Laws about coroners vary from state to state as shown here. Twenty-eight states (dark gray) still have coroners in some or all counties. Some states have limits on how long a person may serve as coroner (Colorado, Idaho, and Indiana). The term of office may be two, four, or six years. The year in which elections are held varies. Some states (Texas and New York) have more than one coroner per county. In Texas, the justice of the peace serves as the coroner. Coroners in Kansas serve districts rather than counties and they are appointed. Coroners are also appointed in Hawaii and North Dakota. Only Ohio, Louisiana, Kansas, and North Dakota require their coroners to be physicians (Louisiana and North Dakota allow nonphysicians if no physician is available). Only eight states have mandated training for their coroners. The best advice is to be thoroughly familiar with the laws and systems that are present in the state in which you live.

Coroners have also been criticized for not requiring autopsies to be performed in a sufficient number of cases, particularly in situations such as infant deaths. You can understand the coroners' position on this when you remember that they are elected local officials. They do not want to upset the people who elect them. Thus, they may be tempted to make decisions that favor their political future rather than making it on the basis of what is the right thing to do at the time. Over the years, however, publicity about such events has reduced this problem substantially, and many of today's coroners are less political than in years past and are more conscientious about their duties to the public. The most important factor is that coroners should be qualified and trained to do the jobs they are asked to do. In some areas this is the case, and in other areas it is not.

11 Medical Examiners

In an earlier chapter it was stated that the title of medical examiner is defined differently in different states. To illustrate these differences, a few specific systems will be described to show how the functions and duties of the medical examiner differ among states.

In Atlanta, GA, there is no office of coroner. The county government appoints a chief medical examiner to investigate deaths that require medicolegal investigation. The laws of the state and county require that the chief medical examiner be a physician with training and experience in pathology, and preferably experience and training in forensic pathology. All deaths in the county that require medicolegal death investigation are reported to the medical examiner's office.

There is a state medical examiner system in Georgia that serves counties with coroners. Medical examiners located regionally throughout the state may serve multiple counties and work with various county coroners. Although deaths are reported to the coroner in each county, they rely upon a regional medical examiner to perform an autopsy and evaluate the medical aspects of the death investigation. State law requires that such people be physicians who have training or experience in pathology. This means that in Georgia, regional medical examiners have a common qualification that they are physicians and that they can perform autopsies.

In North Carolina, the system is basically a county-based medical examiner system with state medical examiner oversight. Nonpathologist medical examiners may assist in death investigations and go to the scene of the death, examine the body externally, collect toxicology samples if necessary, and prepare reports of their investigations, but if an autopsy is needed, the bodies are examined by the state medical examiner or other medical examiner pathologists with training and experience in autopsy and death investigation. The state medical examiner's office is located in Chapel Hill, NC.

In Michigan there is no state medical examiner, but each county has a physician medical examiner. However, these medical examiners need not be pathologists. When the medical examiner is not a pathologist, they must rely on pathologists to perform autopsies when needed. So medical examiners can be physicians who are responsible for documenting the facts of the death investigation but who do not perform autopsies.

In some states the title of medical examiner may be given to persons who are not physicians. Sometimes such persons may work on behalf of a coroner or state medical examiner in collecting information about deaths, conducting scene investigations, and performing other aspects of the investigation except for autopsies. The laws in West Virginia, Wisconsin, and Vermont each permit nonphysicians to be designated as medical examiners.

The Birth of Medical Examiners

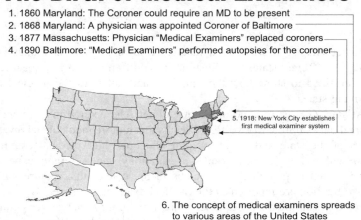

1. 1860 Maryland: The Coroner could require an MD to be present
2. 1868 Maryland: A physician was appointed Coroner of Baltimore
3. 1877 Massachusetts: Physician "Medical Examiners" replaced coroners
4. 1890 Baltimore: "Medical Examiners" performed autopsies for the coroner

5. 1918: New York City establishes first medical examiner system

6. The concept of medical examiners spreads to various areas of the United States

FIGURE 11.1 In 1860, Maryland laws were created that allowed the coroner to require the presence of a medical doctor at coroner's inquests. In 1868 a physician was appointed as coroner of Baltimore. These events marked the beginning of a trend to involve medical doctors in death investigation. The term *medical examiner* was first used in 1877 in Massachusetts when medical examiners replaced coroners. In 1890, the term medical examiner was used to describe the physicians who performed autopsies for the coroner. New York City is credited as having the first real medical examiner system, which was established in 1918. As people trained in New York City, the concept of a medical examiner system was carried with those who moved to other parts of the country, and medical examiner systems gradually began to emerge, replacing the coroner system in some states and counties (see Figure 6.1).

Other names may also be applied to positions that are essentially the same as that of medical examiner. In New Mexico, for example, the chief medical examiner of the state is actually called the Chief Medical Investigator. It should be obvious from this discussion that viewing all medical examiners as being the same in qualifications and experience would be incorrect. It should also be obvious that it is difficult to discuss medical examiners in general because of these variations in definition.

Thus, similar to coroners, medical examiners are a heterogeneous group of individuals with different qualifications and different levels of experience and expertise. The shortage of medically trained people to investigate deaths results in requirements that may not be as strict as they otherwise might be. For example, it might be ideal that all medical examiners be required to be board certified forensic pathologists, but there are simply not enough of them to go around. This means that many medical examiner positions are filled by persons who may have some background or training in pathology, but who may not be board certified or fully qualified. As a result, the quality of death investigations varies.

Medical examiners may approach death investigations differently based on the amount of training they have received, their background experience, and the places they have trained (or not trained!). Many medical examiners, although physicians, are not necessarily affiliated with medical schools or academic institutions. They may simply run an office that is organized by the local government. Thus, their interest in academic issues and scientific issues may not be as great as the interest of other physicians who are engaged in academic centers. Because medical examiner's offices are usually funded by the government, the salaries that are paid to such persons usually rank below the salaries that pathologists might make in other areas of pathology. Thus, medical examiners must be dedicated if they are fully trained and qualified, and willing to accept salaries and income that may not achieve what could otherwise be obtained. Another viewpoint is that the low salaries may attract medical examiners who are not as qualified as some other medical examiners.

When comparing the relative merits and deficiencies of coroners versus medical examiners, the overwhelming concern should center around whether the person who is doing the job is adequately educated, trained, and qualified to do the job he or she is asked to do.

12 Death Investigators

Especially in busy offices, which tend to be located in highly populated areas where large numbers of deaths occur, the medical examiners or coroners cannot conduct all aspects of their investigations by themselves. The coroner or medical examiner may rely on a *death investigator* to assist with the death investigation. The qualifications of these people vary tremendously with the geographic location. There are no standard training or educational requirements for death investigators overall. However, the American Board of Medicolegal Death Investigators (ABMDI), founded in the late 1990s, has developed a standard training curriculum and examination program to become a registered or certified death investigator. A number of death investigation offices now require their investigators to be ABMDI registered or certified.

Death investigators are usually persons with backgrounds in nursing, emergency medical services, the funeral business, or law enforcement, such as police officers. Quite frequently they have taken up death investigation as a second career after having spent some time in another job.

Typically, the medical examiner's or coroner's office is staffed with death investigators who receive initial reports of death. With adequate training, they are capable of making many of the decisions that the medical examiner himself or herself would make, and they often decide what to do with a specific case after taking the initial death report. They collect information from appropriate people about the circumstances leading to death, about the decedent's medical history, and they may conduct a scene investigation. In some offices, they also assist the medical examiner or pathologist with the performance of the autopsy.

Just like coroners and medical examiners, death investigators constitute a diverse group of individuals. The interest and abilities of death investigators vary dramatically.

There are few formal courses in death investigation at the college level. Most death investigators gain their training through on-the-job experience or through the professions they held prior to becoming a death investigator. There are a number of universities and other agencies that periodically hold death investigation courses designed for people who are (or who want to be) death investigators. Usually several such courses are held per year, and a typical course lasts a week. Quite often, the organizers of these educational sessions hold multiple conferences designed for differing levels of experience in death investigation. A major problem is that many of the medical examiner's and coroner's offices do not have sufficient funds to send their investigators to such schools, and the responsibility is often born by the investigator himself. Often, the best that a medical examiner's or coroner's office can do is allow the investigator to take the time with pay to help compensate or offset the cost of such educational courses.

The title of *death investigator* is usually used within medical examiner death investigation systems. In coroner systems, a similar title of *deputy coroner* or *assistant coroner* is often used. However, the duties are quite frequently identical.

13 Who Controls the Scene of Death?

For deaths that require medicolegal death investigation, especially when death occurs outside of a hospital, there is usually a death scene that must be controlled in order to allow an orderly, systematic, and professional investigation, but who has control over the scene of death? Who decides who may come into the scene area and when? And who determines the order in which things are done and who does them?

Control of the death scene is usually described in the death investigations laws of the particular state, and may vary from state to state. In some states the medical examiner or coroner takes charge of the scene, while in others it is the sheriff (or other law enforcement officer). In others, the medical examiner or coroner may have jurisdiction over the body and its immediate surroundings, while the law enforcement agency has authority over the general scene area.

Arguments or disagreements between the medical examiner or coroner and the law enforcement agency sometimes occur at death scenes regarding who is control of the scene or who is in charge of certain parts of the death scene. Usually, however, such disagreements result because one or more of the parties is not familiar with, or does not understand, the law. Disagreements also occur when the medical examiner or coroner and law enforcement personnel haven't worked together before and are unfamiliar with each other's approach to death scenes. Discussion and cooperation are essential. It is common practice, regardless of the law, for the medical examiner or coroner to concern him- or herself primarily with the body and its immediate surroundings, and for the law enforcement agency to secure the scene in general and to concentrate on the parts of the scene that are not in the immediate vicinity of the body.

14 Forensic Scientists

The people who conduct examinations on various types of evidence in death investigations are called *forensic scientists*. The disciplines in the forensic sciences overlap somewhat and have been categorized by different classifications. Although all of them are referred to as sciences, there is an element of art involved, too. Not all analyses are straightforward or can be proven, and results of tests must often be interpreted with opinions, which creates the possibility of a nonscientific approach and errors.

The word *forensic* means "belonging to the courts" or "open to public discussion and debate." Thus, the forensic sciences involve science that has applications in court or in matters of public interest and debate. There are many forensic sciences. In general, the major disciplines involved with death investigation include the following:

- Toxicology
- Criminalistics
- Questioned Documents
- Latent Prints
- Engineering
- Physical Anthropology
- Entomology
- Botany
- Firearms Analysts (Ballistics)
- Serology and Forensic Biology
- Odontology
- Pathology
- Radiology
- Psychiatry/Behavioral Sciences
- Jurisprudence
- Nursing

Each of these will be discussed briefly below, with emphasis on how each discipline is often involved in the field of death investigation.

Toxicology involves the testing of body fluids, tissues, organs, and other substances for the presence of drugs or poisons, or the analysis of compounds to determine their chemical or elemental components. During an autopsy, blood and other fluids are often removed and submitted to a toxicologist for evaluation with respect to the possibility of poisoning or a drug overdose, or to determine the concentration of specific drugs to evaluate whether the person was taking enough of a prescribed medication. Sometimes powders, liquids, or other substances are found at a death scene or on the body of a dead person, and a toxicologist or drug analyst may also test these substances to determine what they are. Testing to see if a white powder is cocaine is one of the more common tests, although there are myriad possibilities. There are many techniques available for performing such tests, but in general, an unknown substance is analyzed in some way to determine its physical or chemical characteristics, and the results are compared with the results of similar tests that are performed on known substances to see how they match. If a specific substance is identified, the amount can also be measured.

Criminalistics involves the analysis of physical evidence such as hairs, fibers, blood stain patterns, footprints, tire treads, and many other objects with the goal of identifying what they are and where they may have come from. The whole discipline is involved in analyzing evidence that may lead to a perpetrator or clarify where, when, or how a death or crime might have occurred. Much of it is based on the theory of *transfer*: when two people or objects interact, there may be evidence transferred from one to the other, or there may be a pattern of some type that can be identified as having come from a specific type or individual instrument, weapon, or object. Analysis may involve trying to place a specific type of evidence into a general class of evidence such as hair, then attempting to describe unique aspects of the hair that can be traced to a specific individual. Criminalists are also involved in the analysis of bombs, explosives, and fire deaths to determine possible causes of such events and to assess whether events may have been accidental or purposeful. For example, the clothing belonging to someone who is found dead in a fire may be analyzed to determine whether gasoline was present, which might suggest that the body was deliberately set on fire.

Questioned documents involve handwriting analysis and evaluation of other evidence that involves documents in some way, usually involving questions of counterfeiting, forgery, or attempting to determine the source of a particular printed document. For example, a questioned document examiner may examine a suicide note and attempt to determine if the handwriting matches the handwriting of the dead person, or if the note was typed on the dead person's computer or someone else's. This science compares an *exemplar*, or known sample, to the unknown sample and looks for points of similarity, identity, or differences, to evaluate the likelihood of whether the known and unknown samples have a common source.

Latent prints generally involve the analysis of residues that are left behind on objects by the ridges on the skin, usually the fingers, but also involving other parts of the body such as the palms and soles. Most people have skin ridges (fingerprints) that are unique to them and different from everyone else. Many techniques are used to make fingerprints more visible, and common methods include dusting with a black powder, the use of lasers that make the prints glow, the use of chemicals such as superglue that can make the fingerprints turn white, and the use of metals or other chemicals that make the fingerprints turn specific colors. Much like other forensic tests, the basic principle involves comparing unknown samples to known samples and looking for points of similarity, identity, and difference.

Engineering involves the analysis of materials and forces. Using mathematical and physical principles, forensic engineers determine answers to questions such as, "how much deformity should occur in a dashboard if a body impacts it when the car is going 60 miles per hour?" or "how much bending would occur in a steering wheel if the car comes to an abrupt stop and a 200-pound driver impacts the steering wheel?" Forensic engineers also reconstruct how physical events might have occurred, for example, they might determine how fast a car might have been going to propel a pedestrian (who was struck) 100 feet through the air.

Physical anthropology involves the examination of bones and other skeletal remains, usually with the goal of determining whether the remains are human or nonhuman, and if human, the age, race, and sex of the individual. The marks and characteristics of bones are also analyzed to determine if the marks occurred before or after death, and whether or not the marks are due to injury, disease, or other events such as gnawing on the bones by animals after death.

Entomology involves the analysis of insects and their by-products to help answer questions about death. For example, certain insects have specific life spans or have lifecycles that are somewhat constant and predictable. A dead body may be found with maggots (insect larvae) on it, the type of maggot may be identified, and the time of death might be estimated from evaluating the stage of life that the maggots were in when the body was discovered. Or the discovery of insects on a body that do not live in the area where the body was found might suggest that the body has been moved. Insects may also be tested for drugs when the body is so badly decomposed (broken down) that adequate tissue does not remain for drug testing.

Botany is similar to entomology except that botanists analyze plant material. For example, a forensic botanist might be able to analyze the roots or leaves of plants that have grown into a dead, buried, body and be able to estimate how long the body has been dead.

Ballistics experts (firearms examiners) primarily analyze guns and bullets. Usually they evaluate whether a gun functions as designed — testing, for example, to see how much force it takes to pull the trigger, and evaluating whether the gun could accidentally discharge. They also examine bullets to determine their type and the type of gun that may have fired them. Firearms analysts sometimes analyze clothing or wounds and wound patterns for the presence of gunpowder and other character-istics to determine the distance between the gun and the target (muzzle-to-target distance). They also analyze samples from the skin to see if gunshot residue is on the hand, for example, suggesting that a person may have fired the gun. Because firearms experts often evaluate patterns or marks on metal such as bullets, many firearms examiners also analyze marks on objects other than bullets for tool marks left by a weapon.

Serology and Forensic Biology involves blood typing and typing of other body tissues, fluids, and unknown substances to determine if they are human, and if so, to whom they might belong. Recently, DNA typing has fallen into the domain of the forensic serologist as it is used for much the same purposes as other blood and tissue typing tests.

Odontology is the science comprising the sum knowledge of the teeth. One major function of odontologists (dentists mainly) in the forensic sciences is to utilize the teeth and dental structures to help identify bodies based on dental records, tooth morphology, and restorations such as fillings. Although the pathologist may do this in many cases, some cases involve very subtle interpretations that require a dentist.

A second major function of odontologists is to analyze bite marks on bodies or other objects in an attempt to match the marks to a specific individual's tooth pattern. Like firearms examiners, odontologists have begun to branch out a little into the area of wound interpretation, which may not necessarily involve teeth, but their role in such cases is controversial.

Pathology is the study of disease (and injury). In death investigation, the pathologist is the one who is usually responsible for examining bodies and human tissue. Forensic pathologists are doctors who have trained in pathology (and usually forensic pathology), and have specific training in autopsy performance, autopsy pathology, and death investigation. Forensic pathology is more thoroughly discussed in Chapter 9.

Radiology involves the application of x-rays and other imaging studies to death investigation. Routine x-rays are often used in death investigations to look for fractures, other injuries, to locate bullets, and to find specific features that may help identify an unidentified person. Often the forensic pathologist can perform and interpret the x-rays. Sometimes, however, the expertise of a radiologist is needed to perform the x-rays or interpret them.

Psychiatry and behavioral science are concerned with analyzing mental and behavioral characteristics, usually of someone who has committed a crime. Forensic psychiatrists may help determine whether an accused person is competent (i.e., not insane) to stand trial. They may also try to analyze the mind of a criminal. Sometimes this is done by interviewing criminals and other offenders to learn their characteristics and thought processes, but sometimes a crime is analyzed in order to get an idea of what the perpetrator might be like, in order to develop strategies for apprehending the offender. For example, they analyze or reconstruct the processes involved in a murder to figure out how long it may have taken to commit a crime, to determine whether the perpetrator may or may not have committed the crime in a familiar, comfortable environment, or to classify whether the crime scene is organized (which may indicate careful thought and planning) or disorganized (which may indicate spontaneity or some forms of mental illness). Forensic psychiatrists may also deal with children who are witnesses to crimes, to help assure that they cope adequately with the experience.

Jurisprudence deals with analyzing laws and legal practices as they relate to evidence, forensic issues, and trials involving forensic science evidence. For example, someone may take an in-depth look at why a particular piece of evidence was not allowed to be admitted as evidence at a trial, and evaluate the possible impact on the case. Jurisprudence professionals may analyze why the outcome of two very similar trials differed, and whether those differences hinged on the judge, the attorneys, or the jury.

Forensic nursing is a relatively new field in which nurses are involved in the management of patients who may be injured or assaulted in some way. For example, in some areas, forensic nurses evaluate children or elderly individuals who are thought to have been abused, or they perform rape examinations and testing on persons who may have been raped or otherwise sexually assaulted. A growing number of forensic nurses have become death investigators or coroners.

In general, the experts in the various forensic disciplines are used on an as-needed basis, and they are not routinely called to work on every case. Toxicology is almost always performed because even if a death was not due to drugs or poisons, the presence of drugs in a dead person may help clarify the circumstances surrounding the death. Criminalists and serologists are involved in most homicide cases. Experts in the other forensic sciences, even in large cities where many deaths occur, may only be used a few times per year depending on need, resources, and the availability of such experts.

Most of the forensic science disciplines have national or regional associations that conduct meetings to share information and to discuss advances in the discipline. The American Academy of Forensic Sciences (AAFS) has members from all of these disciplines, but only toxicology, anthropology, odontology, pathology and biology, criminalistics, engineering, psychiatry and behavioral science, questioned documents, and jurisprudence have specific section meetings at academy conferences. The remaining disciplines have members in the general section of the academy. There is evolving interest in the development of new sections however, such as DNA analysis and digital evidence.

The education and training requirements for the forensic sciences vary depending on the specialty area. There are few schools that have specific forensic science training, and often when such training is available, it does not cover all of the disciplines. As you might imagine, there are fairly obvious requirements for some of the disciplines. Pathologists are, in general, physicians, as are radiologists and psychiatrists; odontologists are dentists; forensic nurses, of course, have some degree in nursing; and those involved with jurisprudence are usually attorneys. All of these professionals first obtain their basic postgraduate degrees and then through additional training or experience, expand their horizons into the forensic world.

The path to the other forensic sciences is less well defined. Usually a bachelor's degree is considered to be a minimal requirement — many forensic scientists have a masters or doctoral (PhD) degrees in a science directly related to the discipline. Toxicology, engineering, anthropology, entomology, and botany are the disciplines that tend to have specific degrees. Remember, when one testifies in court or other legal proceedings, the credibility of the witness is greater if the witness has substantial formal education and experience in the topic area.

Criminalists, questioned document examiners, serology, latent print examiners, and firearms examiners are more diverse in the types of education and training that are required. Again, a bachelor's degree is usually considered to be the minimum level of education for eligibility in these disciplines. However, on-the-job training or a background in police work sometimes provides adequate experience and education. Serologists often have a background in medical technology or lab technology.

If you are interested in the forensic sciences, you may want to contact the nearest crime laboratory in your state and speak with the director to determine the requirements in your area of interest.

Professionally, some of the disciplines have *boards* that establish training requirements for the specialty and offer an examination to show that the applicant has attained at least a minimum level of competence in the field. The forensic sciences that have such boards (or the equivalent) are pathology, odontology, psychiatry, nursing, jurisprudence (law degree with bar exam), radiology, anthropology, and criminalistics. Although these specialties have a board examination, some states

Types of Evidence Commonly Collected
During a Death Investigation

- Blood and tissues for toxicology tests
- Bullets and other foreign bodies found on or in the body
- Hairs and fibers found on the body, possibly associated with perpetrator
- Hairs from the victim for comparison purposes
- Fingerprints
- Paint chips and other foreign material possibly from weapon
- Insect larvae, pupae, and adults to determine possible time of death
- Vegetable/plant material for time of death estimation
- Secretions and stains for DNA profiling
- Photographs of patterned injuries and blood stains
- Scrapings from fingernails for DNA profiling
- Clothing for trace evidence, range of fire, or arson accelerant analysis

FIGURE 14.1 In most cases managed by forensic pathologists, medical examiners, or coroners, the type of evidence encountered will fall into one or more of the categories shown. It is this type of evidence that is collected and transferred to various forensic scientists who analyze the evidence and prepare reports of their analyses.

may not require that the forensic scientist be *boarded*. For many of these specialties, the individual may also be required to be licensed by the state in order to practice, but again, this is not always the case. For example, some pathologists who assist with autopsies may not have to be licensed in the state where they practice, and the same holds true with the other disciplines.

Recently, the American Academy of Forensic Sciences established the Forensic Science Accreditation Board (FSAB) to accredit various programs that offer certifications in various disciplines of forensic science, to help ensure that certification programs are operating appropriately and effectively. The AAFS also has the Forensic Education Program Accreditation Council (FEPAC), which reviews and accredits educational curricula in forensic science to make sure that programs are scientifically based and of good quality.

Figure 14.1 shows some of the more common types of evidence examined by various forensic scientists.

Part III

Goals of Death Investigations

15 Basic Goals of Medicolegal Death Investigation

A major goal of medicolegal death investigation is to ensure that no laws have been broken regarding the death of an individual person, and if they have, that complete information is obtained that can be used to bring violators of the law to justice, and even if no laws have been broken, to evaluate whether the cause of death poses any risk to the public.

The specific practical goals of medicolegal investigation are to determine the cause, manner, and circumstances surrounding death (Figure 15.1). The cause of death relates to the actual disease process or injury that started the chain of events that led to death. For example, did the person die of a heart attack, or did he or she die of internal bleeding due to a stab wound? There are hundreds of such possibilities. The *manner of death* is a classification that relates to the circumstances under which the cause of death occurred. For example, a fatal gunshot wound (the cause of death) may have been intentionally self-inflicted (suicide), intentionally inflicted by another person (homicide), or unintentional (accident) as might occur if a gun is dropped and discharges when it hits the floor. The manner of death is usually determined as being either *homicidal, accidental, suicidal, natural,* or *undetermined.* Homicide, of course, results when a person dies because of an injury or poisoning inflicted by someone else. Usually some degree of intent is required, although this is not universally true. Suicide results when a person dies as a result of a self-destructive act with the intent to do self-harm or produce death. Accidental deaths occur when there is an injury or poisoning that is unintentional and is somewhat unforeseen and unpredictable. Natural deaths are due to diseases and the aging process in which there is no injury or poisoning involved. Occasionally, after thorough investigation, the manner of death cannot be determined and in such instances, the manner of death is regarded as being undetermined.

Medicolegal death investigation is also designed to clarify the circumstances surrounding the death. Common issues include things such as the time of death, the length of time that it would have taken the person to die from the cause that resulted in death, and the place where the events leading to death may have occurred. There are many such possibilities.

Another major goal of the medicolegal death investigation is to obtain evidence. There may be evidence on the body that can be analyzed by other experts to answer some of the questions that come up during a death investigation. Persons who conduct death investigations are trained in the types of evidence that may be important, as

Common Goals of Death Investigation

- Determine the cause of death
- Classify the manner of death
- Clarify circumstances of death
- Collect relevant evidence
- Complete the death certificate
- Prepare official reports of findings

FIGURE 15.1   Death investigation includes some goals that are common to virtually every death that is fully investigated.

well as how to collect it, preserve it, document it, transfer it to appropriate authorities, and on occasion, how to analyze the evidence.

The findings of a death investigation are usually documented in written form, often in several places. For example, the cause and manner of death are usually documented on the *death certificate*. The scene investigation and other investigative details may be filed in an *investigative report* at the medical examiner's or coroner's office. *Police reports* may contain additional information. Laboratory tests, such as those for the presence of drugs and other substances, may be reported by a laboratory that is separate from the medical examiner's office, and again, may be on a separate form and referred to as a *crime lab report*. Usually, however, copies of all these various reports are maintained in some sort of a file at the medical examiner's or coroner's office. These reports are then used by the medical examiner or coroner at a later time if the death results in legal or other proceedings in which the information may be used to resolve the issues that arise.

Quite often, after a medicolegal death investigation, there will be no evidence of the law having been broken. However, the death may have involved issues of civil law in which there is some alleged damage that was sustained by the decedent that caused or contributed to death. Such damages may involve civil lawsuits in which someone is sued to recover damages for causing or contributing to a person's death, such as claims against an automobile manufacturer whose design was flawed or where components of the vehicle were unsafe. In such cases, the information collected by the medical examiner may be very valuable in resolving such issues. In most areas, the possibility of civil law suits does not place the death under the jurisdiction of the medical examiner or coroner in and of itself. However, because many cases investigated by medical examiners and coroners involve injuries or poisonings, there is often an allegation that the death resulted through some fault or noncriminal, but culpable act (*tort*) of another person. The net result is that many cases investigated by medical examiners and coroners end up becoming relevant or important in civil lawsuit procedures.

16 Goals of Institution-Based and Private Death Investigations

The goals of institution-based and private death investigations vary according to the needs of the specific case. Although there may be some routine questions that are answered or addressed in institution-based and private death investigations, usually these investigations are directed at answering specific questions.

For example, consider the case of a person who has been admitted to the hospital with widely spread cancer and who is expected to die in the near future. In a desperate attempt to control growth of the tumor, a relatively new drug is begun and the patient is treated for several weeks but then dies. It may be fairly apparent that the person has died of the complications of the widely spread cancer, but the physicians who treated the patient may be interested in knowing whether or not the medication worked and caused some of the tumor to die. If this information could not be obtained during life by diagnostic tests, an autopsy and death investigation may be necessary to answer such questions.

Quite often, institution-based and private death investigations are performed to determine the cause of death. However, there are numerous other instances in which these types of death investigation may be performed. Such investigations may be performed to evaluate the accuracy of a diagnostic procedure such as an x-ray, to evaluate the performance of an implanted device such as synthetic cardiac valve, or perhaps to remove a device such as a cardiac pacemaker to evaluate whether it is functioning properly. Another example may be to ensure that the surgical suture lines in someone who has had an intra-abdominal operation have remained intact and have not ruptured or caused unexpected hemorrhage. There are numerous such possibilities that may serve as reasons for conducting a death investigation with autopsy.

Private death investigations are also conducted to answer specific questions. Many occur when the circumstances of the death do not qualify the death for medicolegal death investigation, or when a hospital autopsy is not, or cannot be performed. Consider the hypothetical case, for example, in which an elderly relative of yours dies at home after having a long history of high blood pressure. Assume that the death has been reported to the medical examiner or coroner, but because of your relative's age, the medical conditions and lack of any suspicion, the medical examiner or coroner declines to investigate the death. Your relative has not been seen at a hospital recently, and did not die in the hospital (death occurred at home). There is no institution to provide an institution-based autopsy, but you are curious as to whether it was the high blood pressure or something else that caused death. You may be faced with having to hire a pathologist or other individual to conduct a private investigation to determine whether the questions you are asking can be answered, and if so, to conduct a death investigation including possible autopsy to answer these questions. Another example might consist of a case in which you suspect a private nurse of having abused an elderly relative. The medical examiner or coroner investigates the death and finds no cause for concern, but you would like a second opinion. You may have to arrange for a private death investigation to address your questions. Thus, the goals of the institution-based and private death investigations will vary depending on the questions that have been raised at or around the time of death.

Another form of private death investigation is exemplified by what happens in some cases of Alzheimer's disease. You may be concerned that a relative has died of Alzheimer's disease, and you know that this disease can run in families, but you are not sure that your relative actually suffered from Alzheimer's disease. Again, the circumstances of death may be such that there is no opportunity for a medicolegal or an institution-based death investigation. You may have to make private arrangements to have the brain removed and examined by an expert to determine if Alzheimer's disease is really present. There are numerous other situations in which a private death investigation may be desired or required because of such questions.

Part IV

---

*Examples of Death
Investigations by Type*

17 A Typical Institution-Based Death Investigation

To illustrate how a typical death investigation might occur in an institution such as a hospital, let's review a sample case on which we can base the discussion.

Mr. Smith is a 67-year-old man who had no remarkable previous medical history. He began experiencing discomfort in his chest and became weak, and one day the weakness and dizziness was severe enough that he called 911 for emergency services. The emergency personnel responded to the scene and transported Smith to the local hospital. Initial suspicions in the emergency room were that he may have been having a heart attack (myocardial infarction) or possibly some sort of an arterial problem in which the blood dissects along the blood vessel wall (aortic dissection). Unfortunately, about 2 hours after being seen in the emergency room, the patient died before a diagnosis could be made. In the state in question, the death was reportable to the medical examiner because it occurred shortly after admission to the hospital. The death was reported to the medical examiner, but with no indication of foul play and all of the findings indicating that a heart attack was the likely cause of death, the medical examiner declined to investigate the case.

The man's wife had died several years earlier as a result of cancer. His only living relative was a son who was 29 years old. Upon the man's death, the son was asked to come to the hospital and make various arrangements, including a decision about which funeral home would be used for funeral services and burial.

The doctors were somewhat interested in obtaining an autopsy because they weren't sure of the cause of death, although they highly suspected that it was due to a heart attack. The son wanted an autopsy to be performed because he knew that his father had been in good health and had no previous serious medical problems, and was curious as to why he died at this particular time. The son discussed the possibility of autopsy with the physicians, and they agreed that an autopsy would be valuable in this case.

The physicians made sure that the son was indeed the legal next of kin. They asked again if there were any other living relatives, which there were not. The son agreed to take possession of the body for funeral arrangements. Based on this, the physicians felt secure in believing that the son was indeed the legal next of kin and was the person who would be required to give permission to perform an autopsy.

The physicians presented the son with a document called an *authorization for autopsy*. The document explained how the autopsy would be performed, what would be done with the organs and tissues that were removed, and provided a place to indicate if the autopsy was to be limited in any way. An autopsy usually consists of removal and examination of the brain, removal and examination of the neck organs, and removal and examination of the organs in the thorax, abdomen, and pelvis.

However, it is usually within the rights of the person giving consent to limit the autopsy to only certain parts of the body. In this particular instance, the son elected to have a complete autopsy performed and did not apply any restrictions. The doctor also had to sign the form, as did a nurse who witnessed the son's and doctor's signatures.

The son was given a chance to read the consent form, and then it was again explained to him thoroughly by the physicians. He was given a chance to ask questions about specific concerns that he may have had. Along with the autopsy authorization form, the physicians completed another form to send to the pathology department explaining very clearly why the autopsy was being requested. The goal was to determine the underlying cause of death as specifically as possible because it was not known.

Shortly after the man died, his body was transported from his hospital room to the hospital morgue. The death occurred late in the afternoon, and it took most of the remainder of the afternoon and early evening to complete the proper paperwork. The body was held overnight in the hospital morgue and the autopsy was scheduled for first thing the following morning.

Upon the death of the patient, numerous items of paperwork were required to be completed. This included a death report which documented the date and time of death, the potential organ donor checklist to ascertain whether or not the man might have been a suitable organ donor, and a report designating whether or not the patient had any known infectious diseases that might be a hazard to living people. This paperwork and the patient's medical record were transferred to the medical records department where they were photocopied. A copy of the medical record was sent to the pathology department for review in conjunction with the autopsy.

It is usually desirable to review the entire medical record prior to performing an autopsy so that unexpected information or findings can be evaluated and the autopsy guided accordingly. However, this is not always possible, and sometimes the medical record must be reviewed in its entirety or in part after the autopsy is performed. You must remember that when a person dies, the medical record is needed for a number of reasons. The record needs to be reviewed by the physician and a death summary dictated. The medical record is also needed for making lists of the patient's diagnoses for statistical and billing purposes. Quality assurance and risk management committees in the hospital may also want to review the chart to make sure that medical management was appropriate. All of these things happen shortly after death, and there is high demand for the medical record. It is not always possible to obtain the chart (medical record) in its entirety when needed. However, sufficient parts of it are usually available so the pathologist who will perform the autopsy can review basic information related to the case.

The morning following the man's death, the autopsy was performed in the hospital autopsy suite. The examination took approximately three hours. Various samples were obtained to perform some testing that was not done during life. In this particular hospital, which is a teaching hospital, the major organs were kept for teaching purposes and review by other pathologists at a departmental conference. Additional small samples were retained for processing to slides so they could be examined under the microscope for evidence of disease or injury. Additional small pieces of organs and tissues were stored in formalin in case they might be needed at a later date (called *stock tissue*). After the educational autopsy conference, the organs that were no longer needed were cremated at the hospital, and the ones that were valuable for teaching purposes were placed in special containers and placed in a locked storage room. The autopsy authorization form allowed the hospital to keep specimens and to dispose of them when appropriate.

Immediately upon completion of the autopsy, the funeral home designated by the son was notified that the body was ready for release. The funeral home then came to the hospital, signed for the deceased's body, and transported it to the funeral home for subsequent preparation and burial (or cremation).

Following the autopsy, a report was prepared detailing the findings that were visible with the naked eye. Subsequently, this report was amended (updated) with additional information stemming from the lab tests and microscopic examination of the tissues. The entire process took only a few days (in some instances it may take several weeks, and sometimes several months). The College of American Pathologists recommends that all uncomplicated autopsy reports be completed within 30 working days, although certain types of cases may take several months to complete. It is the goal of most institutions to complete their autopsy reports in a much shorter period of time, usually less than one month.

Much of a hospital death investigation involves review of the medical record. There may be very relevant information hidden (not intentionally) in nurses notes, progress notes, laboratory reports, or other parts of the medical record that were not available when the patient died, or that were overlooked in terms of their possible significance. A thorough attempt is made to correlate all of the findings at autopsy with the patient's symptoms, disease manifestations, and lab test results observed during life. In addition, other tests may be performed on specimens taken at autopsy to diagnose abnormalities that were not diagnosed in life.

A hospital-based death investigation also involves personally discussing certain aspects of the case with the patient's physician or other persons caring for the patient while in the hospital. Sometimes things are seen or observed about a patient in a hospital that are not written in the medical record, and talking to people involved in the patient's care may be very informative. Further, the pathologist should discuss the results of the autopsy with the doctors who were caring for the patient.

Ideally, if the patient's physician is responsible for completing the death certificate, it is not completed in its final form until sufficient autopsy results are available. Sometimes the findings observed with the naked eye (*macroscopic* findings, or *gross* findings) during the gross autopsy procedure itself may be enough to allow the signing of the death certificate. However, in many instances, additional tests are needed and the final death certificate must be held as pending. In such cases, a *preliminary death certificate* is filed, which states that identification of the cause of death is pending further investigation, and when the investigation is complete, the death certificate is amended (updated) and the cause of death is placed on the death certificate at that time. This again may take anywhere from several days to weeks or several months or longer, depending on the type of information that is needed.

Often, if the patient dies in the hospital, the family is not charged for the autopsy. The cost of performing autopsies is often born by the hospital in its overhead.

Occasionally, however, the hospital may charge a fee. Be sure to determine if any fees will be charged to you.

The sample case above is one in which both the doctor and a family member showed an interest in obtaining an autopsy. There are additional circumstances in which the hospital-based death investigation may occur, however. Some patients are on treatment protocols with experimental drugs or other substances, and part of the treatment protocol may include the patient giving permission for an autopsy upon death. A few hospitals also allow patients, while they are alive, to give consent for an autopsy to be performed after their death. As discussed in another chapter, the approach of various institutions to this technique differs because many legal authorities still view the body as the property of the next of kin as soon as death occurs.

Usually, when a hospital-based death investigation occurs, the report of the investigation consists primarily of the autopsy report and is filed as part of the patient's medical record. It is typically held as confidential information and cannot be released without the appropriate next of kin's permission. However, it may be used by the doctors or the hospital without specific permission from the family.

It is also wise to remember that the pathologists who perform the autopsies at hospitals and other institutions are usually paid by those institutions, that is, they are on the professional staff of the hospital. Such pathologists are sometimes put in a difficult situation because when they perform an autopsy, they may encounter findings that put the patient's physician or the institution at some potential legal risk for an erroneous act of omission or commission. In other words, the pathologist must occasionally point out to a physician or the hospital that a mistake or suspected mistake or untoward effect may have occurred. Doing so may put the pathologist at odds with the hospital or physician who cared for the patient. Many people recognize this problem and for various reasons, some members of the public do not trust the hospital pathologist to perform an autopsy on a patient who dies in that institution. However, it can be generally stated that such fears and concerns are not usually justified. Most physicians and pathologists recognize the role of the autopsy in evaluating the quality of medical care, and are accepting of objective findings discovered at autopsy or during a hospital-based death investigation. When there is an element of distrust by the family or next of kin regarding the hospital performing the death investigation, the only options are for the family to report the death to the medical examiner or coroner (who may elect not to investigate the death), or to arrange for a private death investigation, or not to pursue the matter any further.

Hospital-based death investigations and autopsies tend to be fairly detailed, and they contain a lot of medical language. Many pathologists who perform hospital or institution-based death investigations have been trained in classical autopsy technique in which the procedure is very methodical and descriptions are done in a very standardized format. This can make autopsy reports very boring to read and difficult to understand. It is important to discuss with the patient's physician or the pathologist, if necessary, any questions that arise when reviewing an autopsy report done in a hospital or other institution. In an autopsy report that stems from an institution-based death investigation, a portion of the report usually contains a summary of the patient's time spent at the hospital and the various symptoms and signs that developed as well as the lab tests that were relevant. This section is analogous to the *investigative report* that comprises part of a medicolegal death investigation described in a later chapter. Also, most institution-based death investigation autopsy reports contain a summary or final comment, sometimes referred to as a *clinical-pathologic correlation* (CPC), where the pathologist expresses opinions about what may have happened to the patient or how a particular disease may have caused or contributed to death or caused the patient's symptoms or signs. This section is analogous to the opinion section that is sometimes included in medicolegal death investigation reports.

Some institutions may not have their own autopsy facility. Usually, however, they have made arrangements with another institution that does have pathologists or an autopsy facility and the body may be transferred to that institution for autopsy. In such cases, procedures would generally be the same as have been described.

If you become involved in providing authorization for the performance of an institution-based death investigation and autopsy, be sure to make all of your questions known prior to performance of the autopsy. In some instances, the questions you may want to have answered may not be answerable by an autopsy and you should be aware of this so that you are not disappointed or have unrealistic expectations. Further, if you make your questions known, the pathologist can specifically address those questions in the autopsy report, if possible.

In some instances, although rare, an institution-based death investigation and autopsy may uncover facts that place the death under the jurisdiction of the medical examiner or coroner. For example, the pathologist at the hospital may find an unexpected hemorrhage around the brain, which may be due to an injury. In such cases, the pathologist is obliged to notify the medical examiner or coroner so they can initiate a medicolegal death investigation, if needed.

An institution-based death investigation usually involves a review of the patient's medical record (chart), the performance of an autopsy or other examination of the body, and discussion of relevant details with the patient's physician and other health care workers. However, it may involve discussions with other hospital personnel, including people who take care of medical equipment such as respirators, oxygen masks, intravenous tubing, and other such experts when potential problems with these items are encountered. Further, findings may be discovered at autopsy or during the death investigation that prompt the pathologist to contact the family to obtain additional information. For example, the pathologist may find a small brain tumor near the nerves that supply the eyes and wonder whether or not the patient may have had any visual disturbances. It may be that the patient did not tell his physician that he had been having difficulties, but when the pathologist discusses this with the wife or other family member, the history is obtained that indeed the patient had been having visual disturbances.

Hospital death investigations may result in subsequent types of investigations or actions. For example, it may be discovered that the patient has some sort of genetic disease that might exist in other family members. Thus, the family members might be notified that genetic counseling is advisable to determine if any other family members are affected with the illness or are likely to develop it in the future. Another example involves the detection of contagious diseases. For example, tuberculosis may be discovered at autopsy. In such cases, state laws often require that the health department be notified so that family members may be evaluated to determine whether they also have tuberculosis or whether they need to be placed on preventative treatment. There are numerous other examples where the hospital-based death investigation may have an impact that goes far beyond the patient who died.

Some institutions have what is referred to as a decedent affairs office, which handles all paperwork and processes that result from a death. This includes many things, such as coordinating activities with the funeral home, evaluating the patient for possible tissue and organ donation, and obtaining permission for autopsy. If a decedent affairs office exists, the procedures are followed in a similar fashion to institutions that do not have a decedent affairs office, except that things are made a little easier because everything is done through one office instead of being fragmented among many different parts of the hospital.

As mentioned at the beginning of this chapter, it is quite often the patient's doctor who asks the family for permission to perform an autopsy, rather than the patient's family asking the physician if one can be performed. However, both approaches are acceptable. Even if the patient's physician does not feel that an autopsy is needed, the family members may find it advisable to request one and may do so by indicating to the physician that they desire an autopsy. Most institutions will accommodate the family's request, as will the physician by signing the autopsy consent form, even if the physician feels that an autopsy is unnecessary.

An institution-based death investigation is enabled by obtaining an authorization for autopsy. Usually the person giving authorization for the autopsy must indicate that he or she is the legal next of kin. In addition, the signature of an additional witness other than the physician who is requesting permission for the autopsy is usually required, as well as specification of any restrictions of the extent of the autopsy being authorized (i.e., limiting the extent).

Institution-based death investigations can be a bargain for the family members of the deceased. As previously described, there is usually minimal or no cost to the family when such investigations occur. Funeral homes will occasionally charge an additional amount when they must do the additional work to prepare the body after autopsy, but this is not common practice.

Finally, it is advisable to specifically ask the hospital if there will be any charges imposed by the performance of the autopsy and death investigation. As previously described, the answer will usually be no. It never hurts to ask, however, in order to avoid unexpected expenses.

In the sample case presented in this chapter, it was determined that the man did die of a heart attack. A copy of the autopsy report was placed in the medical record, a copy was sent to the patient's physician, and a copy was sent to the son who gave consent for the autopsy. The patient's physician completed and signed the death certificate. The son arranged a meeting with the patient's physician, who discussed the autopsy findings with him. It was discovered that the patient had very high cholesterol, so the son also had his cholesterol level checked. His cholesterol level was also very high, so his doctor prescribed some medication and put him on a low-cholesterol diet. Not only did the son find out why his father died, but he discovered that he too had a problem (which he probably inherited), predisposing him to a heart attack, and which needed treatment.

18 A Typical Private Death Investigation

Another case scenario might help explain how private death investigations may occur. For the purposes of this chapter, let us consider the case of a man who comes home from work and finds his wife dead in a chair in the living room. His wife has had a history of severe high blood pressure. Because he is not sure that his wife is actually dead, he calls 911 and the emergency team responds. The police also respond to the 911 call, which is commonly the case. The emergency technicians determine that the woman is dead and do not transport her to the hospital. The policeman feels that he should report this death to the medical examiner because the death occurred outside of the hospital. The policeman calls the medical examiner, but the medical examiner asks a few questions and determines that there is no indication of foul play, there is no evidence of injury, and that the woman had a history of significant high blood pressure for many years and was on numerous blood pressure medications. Thus, the medical examiner declines to investigate the case. The woman has been seeing a private physician for a number of years and has been treated for high blood pressure by him, but she did not die in a hospital. Thus, there is no institution to perform an institution-based death investigation. The woman's husband understands that she may have died of complications of her high blood pressure, but actually she had been feeling fairly well recently and he is curious about why she actually died. What can the husband do? Two options have been ruled out: the medical examiner has declined to investigate the case, and there is no institution to perform an investigation. The only remaining option is for the husband to make private arrangements for an autopsy and death investigation. On whom can he call?

The first thing to do is to contact the patient's physician. That physician may well be aware of a local pathologist who is willing to perform autopsies on a private basis for a fee in cases such as this. If that approach doesn't work, it is not uncommon for the local medical examiner or coroner to be aware of persons who will conduct autopsies and death investigations on a private basis. A call to the local medical examiner or coroner might provide the necessary contact person to make such arrangements. Medical examiners and coroners routinely deal with pathologists who review their work on a second opinion basis, and they usually can refer inquirers to such people when they need assistance.

Another option is to call the local medical society or association. Such organizations often have lists of physicians to whom such matters may be referred.

A fourth option is to contact an attorney. Many attorneys deal with death-related issues and are aware of local pathologists who can perform autopsies and private death investigations. Of course, engaging the services of an attorney may result in a fee. Contacting the patient's physician shortly after death, or the local medical examiner, or coroner for a referral, probably will not result in a fee other than those charged by the person who ultimately performs the autopsy.

A final option would be to contact a private investigator. However, unless there is some suspicion of a crime or foul play, most questions that would need to be addressed in a case such as the one presented would be medical and would be best addressed by a pathologist trained in autopsy pathology performance and reporting. If there was some suspicion of foul play or criminal activity, it is not beyond reason to engage the services of a private investigator who usually has contacts with specific death investigators, such as medical examiners, coroners, pathologists, and the police.

No matter how the arrangements are made to perform a private death investigation, the person performing the investigation and autopsy will probably require a consent form similar to that obtained in an institution-based death investigation. Of course there will, in all likelihood, be a fee charged by the pathologist for performing the autopsy. This may vary from a few hundred dollars to several thousand dollars, depending on the case and the amount of work involved. It also varies considerably depending on the qualifications and expertise of the pathologist.

Quite often, pathologists who perform private death investigations are allowed to use the morgue facilities at the institution where they work. Also, many medical examiner's and coroner's offices make their facilities available for the performance of private death investigations. In some instances, such examinations may have to take place at a funeral home. Where such investigations and examinations are conducted depends on the nature of the case and the facilities that are locally available.

Private death investigations may involve many of the phases that are typical of institution-based and medicolegal death investigations, such as reviewing the medical history, interviewing witnesses, and performance of various lab tests.

The major aspects of private death investigation that make it unique are (1) the investigation is not conducted on behalf of the government or a particular institution, and (2) there will be specific charges for each procedure that is performed, or perhaps a lump sum fee or a fee based on an hourly rate that depends on the time spent by the pathologist or other individual conducting the investigation.

When a private death investigation is conducted, the person giving authorization for the investigation basically owns the report. The person performing the investigation should not give copies to anyone unless the person who has made arrangements for the investigation gives consent. As with any type of death investigation, a private death investigation may uncover findings that put the case in the domain of the medical examiner or coroner. In such instances, the law requires that the medical examiner or coroner be notified. Failure of the pathologist to do so might make him or her vulnerable to legal action for a misdemeanor or criminal offense.

Because they are done on a private basis, private death investigations are generally completed fairly rapidly. They are usually done in situations where paperwork and other details don't tend to get bogged down. The issues are usually fairly well defined, which can guide the investigation in answering specific questions.

A key point to remember is that the next of kin basically owns the deceased's remains. The next of kin should not feel rushed to make funeral arrangements or to transfer the body to a funeral home if additional time is needed to decide whether to pursue a private death investigation. As an alternative, the body may be transported to a funeral home, but the funeral home should be instructed not to embalm or alter the body until a final decision can be made as to what type, if any, of death investigation is to occur. In some cases embalming and body preparation can interfere with the interpretation of autopsy findings, and in general should not be performed until it is clear that all death investigation activities have been completed. In rare instances it is necessary, or sometimes desirable, to embalm a body prior to autopsy, but such circumstances are unusual. If such needs arise, the pathologist should be consulted to determine whether embalming and body preparation will interfere with the goals of the death investigation.

In this particular case, the husband called the local medical examiner's office, and the medical examiner gave him the name of a pathologist who worked at a local hospital. The husband called the pathologist and discussed the case, and the pathologist agreed to perform the examination for a fee of $2,000. The pathologist requested that the husband request and authorize the autopsy in writing, and the funeral home assisted in this process by typing up and witnessing the permission. The body was taken to the hospital by the funeral home, and after the autopsy, the funeral home returned to the hospital, picked up the body, and took it back to the funeral home. The pathologist paid the hospital $200 for use of the morgue facilities and supplies. The autopsy showed that the woman most likely died from her high blood pressure, her enlarged heart probably going into a fatal cardiac rhythm disturbance (abnormal beating of the heart that makes it an ineffective pump). With the husband's approval, the pathologist called the woman's physician and discussed the findings with her. The woman's physician then completed the death certificate, basing her conclusions on the autopsy that was performed. The pathologist prepared a written autopsy report and sent it to the husband, along with his bill for performing the autopsy. The pathologist told the husband that he would not give anyone a copy of the report unless the husband agreed that he should do so, or unless, for some reason, there was a court order to provide someone with a copy.

In this case, the pathologist was working for the husband. In such a case, it is the husband's right to determine how the autopsy findings are used, as long as there is compliance with the law. The husband owns the autopsy report.

19 A Typical Medicolegal Death Investigation

Imagine that your neighbor has just returned home from work and she finds her husband, apparently dead, at the bottom of a flight of steps. She tries to arouse him, but cannot, so she calls 911. Along with the emergency medical technicians, the police also respond as they often do when 911 is called.

Upon arrival of the emergency medical services, the team examines the body for any evidence of life, including a pulse, breathing, or reaction of the pupils. They see no signs of life. In addition, they connect an electrocardiograph machine to the body to see if there is any electrical activity in the heart, and there is none. It is their opinion that the man is dead.

Both the wife and the emergency medical technicians note several small bruises about the face suggesting that there may have been an injury. The policeman who has come to the scene has to file a report that he has responded to a death call. The policeman calls his local precinct and requests that a homicide detective come to the scene, just to be present in case there is some evidence of foul play.

In writing his report, the policeman collects some basic information in which he discovers that the man had not been seen by a private physician for several years. He had no known serious health problems. Because there is evidence of injury, no readily available medical history to explain the death, and no available physician to sign the death certificate, the policeman notifies the county medical examiner's office that this death has occurred. He does this by telephoning the medical examiner's office from the deceased's place of residence.

When the policeman calls the medical examiner's office, he is transferred to a death investigator who then asks some basic questions about the circumstances at the scene and about the decedent. The death investigator learns of the lacking history of any significant medical problems and the presence of a few bruises about the face and decides that he needs to go to the scene of the death. When the death investigator was notified, he assigned a specific case number for reference.

The death investigator takes a small kit with rubber gloves, a tape measure, a camera, some containers for specimens, and other necessary supplies with him and travels in a medical examiner's vehicle to the house where the death occurred. Upon arrival, he again talks with the police officer to gather some information about what he observed and what he had been told.

At this point it is necessary to digress and discuss some of the basic principles of death investigation. The first thing that a death investigator must do upon arrival at the scene of a death is to ascertain that the scene is safe. For example, there may have been a carbon monoxide leak in the house, which may pose a risk to other persons who are still alive. The investigator must ensure that everyone who will be processing the scene of the death will be as safe as possible. This may involve calling in experts from the gas company or other agencies to conduct tests to determine that the scene is safe.

The next important function is to secure the scene. That is, to make sure that no unwanted people have access in and out, and that contamination and walking around at the scene will be held to a minimum. This may actually involve the setting up of some sort of a barricade, usually using some sort of plastic ribbon that is stretched around the house or around a specific room to keep people from going in and out unless they have business there. The services of additional police officers may be needed in some instances to secure the scene.

In this particular instance, the death investigator has with him a small apparatus that can test carbon monoxide levels in the air; he performs the test and the air is safe. There is no other evidence of any sort of immediate danger that he feels necessary to evaluate. As a result, he begins to conduct his investigation at the scene.

Because there is no evidence of homicide at this point, the homicide detective who was called to the scene primarily stands by and observes while the death investigator carries out his or her business. Usually, if the police do need to conduct their own investigation of the scene, the medical examiner or coroner concerns him- or herself primarily with the body and the objects immediately in contact with it, and the police agency concerns itself with the surroundings, such as the room and other areas of the house, which they may search and examine for evidence. In this particular case, the death investigator feels initially that there is no need to thoroughly process the scene because there is no evidence of a crime having been committed.

The death investigator examines the body to estimate approximately how long the body has been dead. In talking to the decedent's wife, he discovers that the man had a conversation with his wife on the telephone at approximately 3:00 PM. As far as anybody knows, that was the last time he was known to be alive, and she discovered him near the staircase at approximately 6:00 PM when she returned from work. The changes on the body are consistent with the body having been dead only about an hour or so, as rigor mortis is absent, livor mortis (the settling of blood in the body) has just begun, and the body is still warm to the touch. So far, the findings on the body are consistent with the statements of witnesses.

One of the major functions of the death investigator at the scene is to document the nature of the scene. This may be done with photographs, diagrams, videotapes, or any combination of these. It is important that the death investigator document findings as soon as possible and before the body has been moved or the scene has been altered, if possible.

After the position of the body has been well documented, the death investigator proceeds to examine the body more closely and does notice that there are several small scrapes and bruises about the face. These do not appear to be too serious and are consistent with the man having banged his head or face on the stairs or floor at the bottom of the staircase. He notices that the body is lying face down, with the feet closest to the stairs, suggesting perhaps that the decedent was coming down the stairs rather than going up the stairs.

A critical part of the investigation is the interviewing of witnesses. Much of this may be done at the scene of the death, but a substantial portion may be done afterward by personal or telephone interviews as well. In this particular case, while the death investigator is at the scene and the wife is available, he discusses the decedent's history with her and discovers that to the best of anyone's knowledge, the decedent did not have any serious medical problems, he had not been depressed, he had never mentioned or talked about committing suicide, and he had been in his usual state of health on the day he died. The death investigator collects information about the man's occupation and his usual activities, especially those within the past day or so prior to death. After discussing this with the wife, absolutely nothing seems out of the ordinary.

The wife has told the death investigator that the deceased had not been on any medications. The death investigator examines the medicine cabinet in the bathroom and does find some antacid tablets, with evidence that some had been used. This prompts the death investigator to ask the wife who was taking these antacids and why. She then replies that her husband had been having some heartburn lately and had gone to the pharmacy several days earlier to buy some over-the-counter antacids. She had forgotten to mention this earlier because she was thinking in terms of prescription drugs, and did not think about things that the man may have bought at the drug store without a prescription.

The death investigator also discovers that the man is essentially independently wealthy and is semiretired, although he is only 54 years of age. On this particular day, he had chosen not to go to work because one of his associates was handling all of the business that needed to be handled on that day and he didn't feel "up to snuff." There was evidence on the kitchen counter that he had eaten lunch, and there was an empty can of chicken noodle soup in the trash can with a partially opened bag of crackers on the counter. The newspaper was spread out on the table as though the deceased had been reading it.

The death investigator also documents the general layout of the house and area of the body with a diagram and photos and notes that the bathroom in which the antacids were kept is on the upper level of the home and the deceased would have had to go up the steps to obtain the antacids if he wanted them.

After conducting his scene investigation, the death investigator informs the emergency medical technicians that they may leave and that the police officer is no longer needed. There is no evidence of any criminal activity, so the homicide detective leaves as well. The death investigator telephones a local body transport service that comes to the house to collect the body for transport to the county morgue. Prior to transport, the body is placed on a clean white sheet and is placed in a body bag so that it is protected during transport and any potential evidence or objects on the body will remain in place.

In some areas, the pathologist who will be performing the autopsy routinely goes to the scene of death when a scene investigation is conducted. However, that is not the usual case, and more often a person such as a death investigator, acting on behalf of the medical examiner, coroner, or pathologist, goes to the scene and conducts the investigation as was done in this case. However, most death investigation offices have the ability to call a pathologist to the scene if one is needed to make some initial assessments about what may have happened. Sometimes the nature of a death is not clear, and the presence of a pathologist may be very helpful in order to inform the police as to whether further investigation is needed. It should also be noted that a scene investigation is not always conducted. Although the medical examiner's or coroner's office may be notified, they may be able to collect sufficient information over the telephone, relying on the police, emergency medical technicians, or the patient's doctor to collect adequate information to rule out foul play, criminal activity, or injury. When there is any doubt, however, a scene investigation is usually conducted. In this case, the lack of a medical history and the finding of the body at the bottom of a flight of stairs with apparent injuries were enough to warrant a scene investigation. This is particularly true because the decedent was only 54 years old.

After being picked up at the scene by the body transport service, the body is transported to the county morgue facility. When the death investigator gets back to the office, he completes some standard forms that contain specific pieces of information about the death in question. This form is presented to the medical examiner or pathologist to review so a decision can be made as to whether to conduct an autopsy, and if so, the extent of examination to be conducted. In some instances an external examination of the body will suffice. In others, a complete autopsy is necessary. In still others, it may be adequate to inspect only certain parts of the body. However, the preferred method in most cases is to conduct a complete autopsy, particularly when the cause of death is not known and the circumstances indicate no obvious cause of death.

In this particular instance, the pathologist decides to do a complete autopsy. The examination takes approximately 1.5 hours and involves an assistant who helps the pathologist remove the organs for examination and prepare the body for transport to the funeral home.

Establishing the cause and manner of death was quite simple after the autopsy was performed. In fact, no subsequent tests were even really required to determine the cause and manner of death. Several antacid tablets were in a pants pocket. The pathologist could see with his naked eye that the coronary arteries that supply the blood flow to the heart were severely blocked with atherosclerosis (hardening of the arteries) and a small thrombus (a coagulated mass of blood) had completely blocked one of the arteries that supplies the heart, causing a part of the heart muscle to die. This is commonly known as an acute myocardial infarction (heart attack). The appearance of the infarction looked as though it had been going on for a number of hours or perhaps a day or so. This may explain why the decedent had been taking antacids as the pain from a heart attack often mimics indigestion. The man apparently collapsed while coming down the steps. Thus, in this case, the pieces of the puzzle fit together very nicely. The autopsy was also important in that it showed that there were no significant internal injuries. The small bruises and marks on the face resulted from when the man collapsed on the stairs but did not cause any significant injuries or contribute to death in any way. Because death was due to a natural disease process, the blockage of the arteries, and no injury was involved, the manner of death was classified as natural.

As soon as the autopsy was conducted and the body was cleansed and prepared for transport, the funeral home that had been selected by the decedent's wife was notified and they came to the morgue and picked up the body, took it to the funeral home, and embalmed it and prepared it for funeral services and burial.

In this particular medical examiner's office, the medical examiner who conducted the autopsy dictated his findings as he went along. He also prepared some handwritten notes and diagrams and took some photographs during the procedures. As soon as the autopsy was complete, the dictation was given to a transcriptionist who processed his words into a typewritten report.

The very same day, because the cause of death was very clear cut and obvious, the medical examiner completed his portion of the death certificate and certified the cause of death as acute myocardial infarction due to atherosclerotic coronary artery disease. He also certified that the manner of death was natural. The death certificate was given to the funeral director, who then completed the other portions of the death certificate, and the following day filed it with the county vital records registrar. The following day the medical examiner also proofread the draft of his autopsy report, corrected it, and the transcriptionist made appropriate corrections. Three days later the pathologist reviewed the tissue sections microscopically and added written findings to the autopsy report. The transcriptionist prepared the final report, and the medical examiner signed it the following day and dated the case as being complete five days following the death. This case was completed more quickly than some cases that require toxicology or other information, which may take time to collect.

It should be noted that the amount of time taken to complete reports varies dramatically from office to office. Some death investigation offices are much better staffed than others, and do indeed have a one- or two-day turnaround time on reports. Others however, may take weeks to finalize their reports. Also, the length of time required to complete a case depends on how much testing is needed following the autopsy. For example, if it is necessary to wait for drug testing and other tests that may be needed, it may take weeks to months to obtain all the necessary information to finalize the report.

In the case presented here, the medical examiner collected routine blood and urine samples for drug testing. About three weeks following the autopsy examination, the toxicology results became available and they were negative for alcohol and common drugs.

A copy of the police report made by the police officer who responded to the scene was obtained from the police department and kept in a file folder at the medical examiner's office, which also contained the investigator's report completed by the death investigator, the pathologist's autopsy report, and the results of the drug tests performed by the crime laboratory in the area. In this office, these records are kept in the medical examiner's office for approximately five years and are then sent to the county archives building where they are maintained indefinitely. At some point in the future, they may be scanned into a computer for permanent storage in electronic form. The electronic versions of the various reports are maintained on a computer server at the medical examiner's office and are backed up onto the county's computer system.

In the particular state in which this death occurred, medical examiner records are considered public information and anyone can obtain a copy of the report.

However, some states have stricter confidentiality laws and restrict release of the report to the dead person's immediate family or only to persons who have a legitimate interest in the case. Such practices vary from state to state.

Most states also have a provision that even if the medical examiner's records are considered public records, they may be withheld from the public if there is an ongoing investigation. For example, if someone is murdered and the case has not yet been solved, releasing the report prematurely may jeopardize the investigation. Thus, most states have laws that enable the medical examiner to withhold information if indeed an ongoing investigation may be jeopardized. The decedent's wife, of course being concerned about what happened, contacted the medical examiner's office. She was connected by phone with the pathologist, who discussed his findings with her and explained as best he could what caused her husband's death. In some instances the pathologist may meet personally with family members or other interested parties to explain the results of a death investigation. How such communication is conducted depends on the office.

A number of offices will send a letter to the next of kin or the decedent's family explaining in layman's terms what happened to the decedent. It is very difficult for a family member to pick up an autopsy report, read it, and understand it. Further, it contains medical terminology and descriptive terms that may not be pleasant or easy to read. For these reasons, many medical examiner's or coroner's offices will create a separate document that explains, in nonmedical terms, the cause and manner of death. Again, however, the practices of various medical examiner's and coroner's offices vary depending on staffing and personal philosophies.

In most areas there are no charges to the family as a consequence of a medicolegal death investigation. However, as previously mentioned, some funeral homes charge an additional amount if an autopsy has been performed because of the additional work required for body preparation. Also, in a few offices where the budget is tight, there may be a charge for body transport. The rule of thumb is, however, that a medicolegal death investigation will not result in any charges to the family.

If there was a coroner in the county where this death occurred, it would have been the coroner who was notified of the death, and most likely the coroner would have gone to the scene and conducted the examination as did the investigator in this example. The coroner would then have notified a local pathologist, medical examiner, or coroner's pathologist to request that an autopsy be performed. The person who performed the autopsy would then inform the coroner of the results, and the coroner would complete and sign the death certificate. The coroner would most likely have a file in which all of the investigative reports, including the autopsy report, are kept.

If a crime had been committed, copies of the autopsy and death investigation reports would have been sent to the district attorney, who could then use them during the legal process for presentation to the grand jury and at trial, if necessary. Discussion of criminal law procedures is beyond the scope of this book. Had a communicable infectious disease such as tuberculosis been discovered, the health department would have been notified. Had a genetic or inheritable disorder been found, the family would have been advised that genetic counseling or examination by a physician may be advisable.

20 Death Investigation: The Rake Analogy

Although highly publicized court trials have made the public more aware of some of the limitations, inconsistencies, and weaknesses in the death investigation system, many people still lack a basic understanding of how death investigation works. Television shows such as *Quincy*, *Crossing Jordan*, *CSI*, and others have also created a false perception on the part of the public regarding the specific roles played by the forensic pathologists, medical examiner, or coroner. People tend to believe that once the medical examiners or coroners get the body, they do the bulk of the investigation and are involved in many aspects of solving the case. However in reality, work is often split up among many people who do small portions of the investigation, which taken together create the sum total of the investigation.

To visualize this process, a *rake analogy* can be used. Imagine a lawn rake like the one you use to rake leaves in the fall. The top of the handle represents the point at which a dead body is found or death occurs. The handle of the rake represents the time between death and the time at which the pathologist or medical examiner receives the body for examination. As time proceeds downward along the handle of the rake, a number of events might happen. Emergency medical services, the police, and a medical examiner or coroner may come to the scene of the death and examine the body in its surroundings. If a crime or suspicious death is involved, there may be crime laboratory personnel or other forensic technicians who come to the scene and collect evidence and prepare photographs. The body may be transported from one location to another. Ultimately, if the body is to be examined at a morgue, the pathologist, medical examiner, or other physician who will examine the body does so at the point represented by the junction of the rake handle and the prongs of the rake (Figure 20.1).

The person who examines the body must be able to recognize various types of evidence and collect it for transmission to other forensic science experts. The autopsy or examination of the body may be the last point at which the body itself is examined prior to transfer to a funeral home for preparation and burial. Specimens and evidence may be collected and passed on to a number of other people for subsequent examination and analysis long after the body is transported to the funeral home and buried.

Imagine that each of the prongs on the rake represents a pathway from the pathologist to a specific type of expert. One prong may represent a path to a toxicologist, another may represent a path to a serologist, another may represent a path to a firearms examiner, and so on.

Thus, contrary to the popular beliefs of many, the pathologist examines the body and collects different types of specimens and evidence, but then "passes the buck" (along with the evidence) to other specialists who assist in the investigation. Thus,

The "Rake" and "Wheel" Analogies

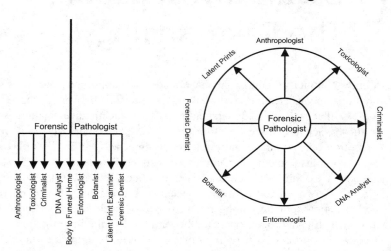

FIGURE 20.1 The forensic pathologist's role may be better visualized with the *rake* or *wheel* analogy. When death occurs, the body is examined by the forensic pathologist prior to its release to the funeral home. While the forensic pathologist is examining the body, he or she collects various types of evidence which are then passed on the appropriate forensic scientist(s) for further analysis. Thus, the forensic pathologist is the final common pathway for collection of evidence from the body and for communicating with other forensic scientists about the case. Whether you prefer the rake or the wheel diagram, each one makes clear the central and key role of the forensic pathologist in case management.

by the time a case comes to trial or is used in other legal proceedings, the testimony or opinions of many people may be involved. The forensic pathologist is not the only character in the investigation, and quite often the key information that helps solve crimes or assists in the prosecution or defense of a case rests with experts other than the forensic pathologist or physician examining the body itself.

Some might prefer to imagine these relationships as being illustrated by a wheel rather than a rake, with the pathologist in the center of the wheel, and the spokes leading outward to the other forensic scientists who are all connected through communication by the rim of the wheel. However, there is not always feedback and communication among all of the experts involved in a case. Results may not be fed back to, or be relevant to the pathologist. For example, the pathologist may obtain a tube of blood and pass it on to the serologist at the crime lab for DNA profiling. When the case comes around for trial, the DNA profile may not be relevant to what the pathologist must testify about, and it may be the serologist who testifies in court about the victim's DNA and how it relates to the other facts and evidence in the case. Thus, the pathologist hands off the evidence and may have nothing more to do with it, making the rake analogy more applicable than the wheel analogy.

The rake analogy can be applied to any of the three basic types of death investigation. Medicolegal death investigations, institution-based death investigations, and private death investigations all usually involve the need to analyze specimens or evidence that is beyond the expertise of the pathologist. For example, in a hospital-based death investigation, there may need to be laboratory tests that are performed in addition to the autopsy. In a medicolegal death investigation, many of the forensic science experts described elsewhere in this book may be involved. Even in private death investigations, a person who is conducting the investigation may need to solicit the services of other experts to answer questions that arise during the investigation.

The main point to remember is that death investigation often represents a complex interaction among many people with different areas of expertise. Although the activities may be coordinated through the medical examiner, coroner, or pathologist, their opinions and findings may ultimately be based considerably on the opinions of other experts and forensic scientists, and in some instances the findings of such experts may not be relevant to the role of the coroner, medical examiner, or pathologist.

The time lapse that occurs between the start of a death investigation and its end can vary dramatically. Many are completed within a day or less, while others may take weeks or months. Occasionally a death investigation may take years. Not all phases of the investigation are completed at the same time. For example, the examination of the body and collection of all of the evidence and specimens may be done within a few hours, yet it may take the toxicologist several weeks or months to complete his or her portion of the examination. If the medical examiner's or coroner's findings must rely upon such tests, completion of the death investigation may be delayed considerably for reasons that are beyond his or her control. The medical examiner or coroner often gets blamed for taking too much time in an investigation, when in fact it is often not really the medical examiner's or coroner's fault.

Part V

Specific Features of Medicolegal Death Investigations

21 What Types of Deaths Are Reportable to the Medical Examiner or Coroner?

You will remember that the types of death required by law to be reported to the medical examiner or coroner vary among states. However, there are enough similarities between the laws that some generalizations can be made.

The Model Postmortem Examination Act of 1954 basically sets out several categories of death that should be reported to the medical examiner or coroner. These include the following:

1. Any death that is known or suspected to have resulted from violence (including injury or poisoning of all types)
2. Any death that involves a potential public health threat such as contagious disease
3. Sudden deaths not caused by readily recognized disease
4. Deaths of inmates of public institutions not hospitalized therein for disease
5. Deaths resulting from occupational disease or injury

Many states have changed the language in their laws to include more descriptive terminology or other types of death such as accidents, violent deaths, deaths that are thought to have resulted from attempts at criminal abortion, and numerous other categories. The net result, however, is that most states have laws that require deaths that are known or suspected as having resulted from any type of injury or poisoning, or which are sudden, unexpected, and unexplained be reported to the medical examiner or coroner (Figure 21.1). That's the long and the short of it.

For the specific language in various state laws, it is necessary to consult the state laws themselves, or for a capsule summary, see information on the CDC Medical Examiner/Coroner web site at http://www.cdc.gov/epo/dphsi/mecisp/index.htm keeping in mind that the information is not always current.

Many deaths fall into a gray zone in which it is not exactly clear whether the death is required to be reported to the medical examiner or coroner. In such cases, it is prudent to report the death to the medical examiner or coroner and let them decide whether or not a death investigation is needed — for example, when someone dies during a surgical procedure that in and of itself may not place the death under the jurisdiction of the medical examiner or coroner. However there is the possibility during some surgeries that there may have been an injury or adverse toxic reaction

Types of Death Investigated

- Death is known or suspected as having resulted from injury or poisoning (external conditions)
- Death is sudden, unexpected, and not explained with reasonable medical probability
- Deaths of inmates of jails or state institutions, or while in the custody of law enforcement agencies
- Death occurs under unusual or suspicious circumstances
- Death occurs and there is no physician to complete and sign the death certificate.

FIGURE 21.1 Although the death investigation laws of each state vary somewhat from those of other states, there are certain types of deaths that are investigated in virtually every state, as shown here. Whether or not other types are investigated, such as deaths during anesthesia, possible medical malpractice, conditions of potential public health importance, and others, depends on state law.

that resulted in the patient's death, and that may place the death under the jurisdiction of the medical examiner or coroner. Quite often in such cases, the medical examiner or coroner must use his or her professional judgment to determine whether the facts of the case warrant an investigation or not.

The laws of most states do not require that the medical examiner or coroner accept the case once it is reported to them. The law simply requires that certain types of cases be reported, and then the medical examiner or coroner determines whether or not an investigation will occur, and if so, the extent of the investigation. These case-specific variables, as you might imagine, can cause some inconsistencies from place to place in the types of deaths that are investigated, and also variation in the extent of investigation that is conducted.

If you have further interest in what takes place in your own neighborhood, you may call your local coroner's or medical examiner's office and ask them what types of death are required by your local laws to be reported to the medical examiner or coroner.

Most laws require that *any person* who has knowledge of a death that may be subject to medicolegal death investigation report the death to the medical examiner or coroner. Because of the way deaths occur, this is usually done by emergency medical personnel who respond to the report of an injured or dead person, or by the police who often respond to death scenes. However, it is possible that none of these agencies may be involved when a death occurs, or they may neglect to report it. Thus, on occasion it may be necessary for a family member to report a death to the medical examiner. Most laws provide for the assessment of some fine or other penalty if it can be shown that a death was intentionally not reported by a person who should have reported it, although the enforcement of these laws is rare.

If you ever have a question about whether a death may be reportable to the medical examiner or coroner, you can call the medical examiner or coroner to find out if it has been reported, and if you wish to report it, you can report it directly to the medical examiner or coroner. Remember, however, that in general, you should do this only if you suspect an injury, poisoning, or foul play, or if the death is sudden, unexpected, unusual, or without an apparent cause or reasonable explanation.

22 Examples of Medicolegal Death Investigation Systems

Several examples of the different types of death investigation systems are presented below in order to understand the scope of their variation.

The most common type of medicolegal death investigation system can be described by using the Ohio example. In Ohio there are 88 counties, each of which has its own death investigation system. Each county has a person who is officially responsible for conducting medicolegal death investigations, and in those counties that person is called the coroner (except in Summit County, which has a medical examiner system). Although the coroners in the counties in Ohio must be physicians, most are not pathologists and cannot conduct autopsies. When a reportable death occurs, the coroner is notified and conducts an investigation. However, if an autopsy is needed, he or she may rely on local pathologists or forensic pathologists to conduct autopsies for them. Some cities and counties, such as Franklin County (Columbus, Ohio) and Hamilton County (Cincinnati, Ohio) have dedicated physical facilities out of which the coroner operates. These facilities house forensic pathologists and other pathologists to conduct autopsies. Many of these pathologists work full time for the coroner. However in smaller counties, which may not even have a hospital, the coroner may have to rely on nearby hospital pathologists or other persons who may be located in different counties to conduct autopsies or examinations of bodies when needed. The death investigation system is not organized on the statewide level, and there is no state agency that collects the death investigation information from all 88 counties. Each county maintains its own information. Every four years, when elections occur, a new coroner may be elected and procedures may change slightly. Many states that have similar types of systems in which death investigations and record keeping are maintained at the county level. This type of system has advantages in that death investigation services are based locally, which means there is someone in relatively close proximity that can investigate deaths. There are, however, disadvantages due to the large number of people involved, which makes statewide coordination of services difficult. Consistency in quality from one county to another may also be difficult to achieve. Further, many of the people conducting the death investigations may not be specifically educated, trained, or experienced in the field of death investigation.

On the opposite end of the spectrum is the state of New Mexico, where the Office of the Chief Medical Investigator (OCMI), located in Albuquerque, conducts all medicolegal death investigations in the state. The office is notified of medicolegal cases that occur throughout the state, and the bodies are transported to Albuquerque where the autopsies or other examinations of the body are conducted by forensic pathologists. The records of all medicolegal death investigations in the state are maintained in one office. Staff consists of full-time forensic pathologists who are trained and experienced in the field. This type of system, however, has the disadvantage that it covers a very large area and that the pathologist or trained medicolegal death investigators may not be able to go to all death scenes in which it would be nice to have a death scene investigation, especially by a pathologist. There are no coroners in New Mexico. All death investigations are conducted by forensic pathologists or other pathologists under the auspices of the forensic pathologists.

Somewhere between the Ohio and New Mexico models is the New Jersey model. A state medical examiner's office exists in Newark, but this office does not conduct all of the death investigations in the state. There are, throughout the state, several regional medical examiner's offices that serve multiple counties. The records resulting from the death investigations in the regional offices are forwarded to the state offices, so there is some state oversight of death investigation activities, and all regional medical examiners are responsible to the state medical examiner in Newark. This system has the advantage that there is coordination at the state level, but has the disadvantage that regional practices may vary somewhat, based on the qualifications of personnel and the resources available. Similar to New Mexico, there are no coroners in New Jersey. Death investigations are conducted by physicians (usually pathologists) who can perform autopsies.

The state of Georgia serves as a fourth example. There are 159 counties in the state and 154 of them have a county coroner; the other 5 counties have abolished the office of coroner and have medical examiner systems. In Georgia, coroners do not have to be physicians, and the requirements are mainly those one must have to be eligible to hold elective office. The medical examiner's offices, as might be imagined, exist in the metropolitan Atlanta area and are staffed by trained forensic pathologists who have specific autopsy and death investigation facilities. In many of the other counties and cities throughout the state, the coroner's offices may not exist as a specific physical facility, and the coroner's duties may be conducted out of the coroner's home or other business in which the coroner happens to be engaged. A copy of all death investigations, at least for injury deaths, is filed at the state level, however. The death investigation records are maintained at the Georgia Bureau of Investigation (GBI). Autopsies are done for the coroners in Regional GBI Division of Forensic Sciences crime labs, which have morgues, and which are staffed by trained forensic pathologists who serve as regional medical examiners. A state medical examiner in Atlanta oversees these regional medical examiners.

There is no federal agency that routinely collects medicolegal death investigation records from the 50 states. Although some national data collection programs have been established for selected types of death, there is no national repository for complete death investigation information on all deaths.

23 Types of Medicolegal Death Investigation by State

Below, listed alphabetically by state, is descriptive information about the type of medicolegal death investigation system in each state. Each state can be classified as a coroner, medical examiner (ME), or mixed state. Coroner states have coroners in every county and lack medical examiner systems. Medical examiner states have no coroners. Mixed states have at least some coroners, but also have at least one medical examiner system. Figures 23.1 through 23.4 show death investigation types and their historical emergence in the U.S.

Alabama (mixed). Most of the 67 counties in Alabama are served by elected coroners who do not need to be physicians to qualify for office. A few of the larger counties have physician medical examiner systems in which the medical examiner is appointed — those counties do not have elected coroners. The coroners around the state rely on regionally (district) based physician medical examiners to conduct autopsies and bodily examinations when needed. Such medical examiners work with coroners from several counties. The district medical examiners are typically based in larger cities, such as Birmingham, Mobile, Montgomery, Tuscaloosa, and Huntsville. The medical examiner districts are administered through the Alabama Department of Forensic Sciences.

Alaska (ME). In the past, the 14 organized boroughs and unorganized regions were served by four district coroners who were elected district judges or magistrates and served as *ex officio* coroners. A judge could appoint a public administrator to serve as coroner. The coroners were supported by eight district medical examiners' offices in the larger cities such as Anchorage, Fairbanks, Juneau, and Ketchikan. A state medical examiner in Anchorage now oversees the medical examiner activities in the state and there are no longer any coroners.

Arizona (ME). The 15 counties in Arizona are each served by county-appointed physician medical examiners who are, preferably, skilled in forensic pathology. The system is not organized on a statewide basis with oversight by a single state medical examiner. There are no coroners in Arizona.

Arkansas (mixed). Each of the 75 counties in Arkansas is served by an elected coroner who need not be a physician. These coroners rely upon a state-appointed, physician-state medical examiner, based in Little Rock, for the performance of autopsies and bodily examinations. The state medical examiner must have training in forensic pathology.

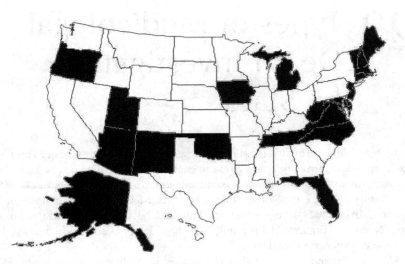

FIGURE 23.1 The states shown in black do not have coroners. In each state shown in white, there are coroners in some or all counties. Coroners are usually elected, and they are not required to be physicians. However, coroners are required to be physicians in Ohio, Kansas, Louisiana, and North Dakota. Also, the coroners in Kansas serve districts rather than single counties, and the coroners in Kansas and North Dakota are appointed rather than being elected. In some states such as California, the sheriff may serve as coroner, and in Nebraska, the elected county attorney serves as coroner. It is fairly accurate to say that each state has some unique feature about its death investigation system that makes it different from other states. See Figure 6.1 for further details.

California (mixed). The 58 counties in California are served by various types of systems. The system is not organized on a statewide level; rather, each county runs its own system. Some counties are served by a county coroner who is elected in some counties and appointed in others, and need not be a physician. Other counties are served by an elected county sheriff-coroner who also need not be a physician. Still other counties are served by a county-appointed, physician county medical examiner, who must be qualified as a specialist in forensic pathology. The counties served by coroners or sheriff-coroners have access to pathologists who can perform autopsies and bodily examinations when needed.

Colorado (coroner). Each of the 63 counties in Colorado is served by an elected coroner who need not be a physician. These coroners rely upon pathologists to conduct autopsies and bodily examinations. In general, the pathologists are based in the larger cities throughout the state.

Connecticut (ME). The eight counties in Connecticut are served by a state-appointed, state medical examiner with state office operations in Farmington. There are no coroners in Connecticut. The state medical examiner must be a board certified forensic pathologist. All medicolegal death investigations are managed through the state office.

Delaware (ME). The three counties in Delaware are served by a state-appointed state chief medical examiner based in Wilmington, who must be a board certified

Counties served by a medical examiner system	Counties
State Medical Examiner System; No Coroners (19 states) AK CT DE IA MA MD ME NC NH NJ NM OK OR RI TN UT VT VA WV	697
Medical Examiner System in every County (2 states) AZ MI	98
District Medical Examiner System; No Coroners (1 state) FL	67
Sporadic County Medical Examiner Systems (14 states) AL CA CO GA HI IL MN MO NY OH PA TX WA WI	98
Total Counties in the United States	3137
Total Counties Served by a Medical Examiner System	960 (31%)

FIGURE 23.2 About one-third of the counties in the United States are served by medical examiner systems, although about half of the population is served by medical examiner systems, which tend to be located in larger cities. This figure shows which states have medical examiners, and whether they are organized on the county, district, or state level.

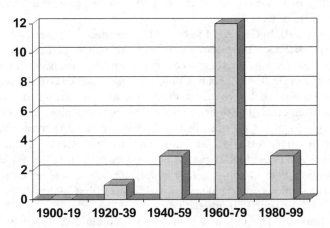

FIGURE 23.3 State medical examiner systems began to emerge prior to 1940 and most were developed between 1960 and 1980.

pathologist, preferably with training and experience in forensic pathology. There are no coroners in Delaware. All medicolegal death investigations in the state are conducted through the state office.

District of Columbia (ME). The District of Columbia is served by a chief medical examiner who is a pathologist. There are no coroners in the district. All medicolegal death investigations are conducted through a single office.

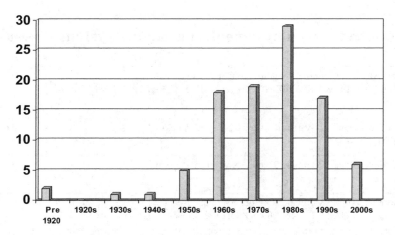

FIGURE 23.4 The development of county medical examiner systems (including districts) took off in the 1960s, peaked in the 1980s, and has declined somewhat in the past two decades.

Florida (ME). The 67 counties in Florida are divided into 24 districts, each of which is served by a medical examiner who must be a practicing physician specializing in pathology. A medical examiner commission oversees death investigation policy, but each district is somewhat autonomous and there is no state medical examiner. There are no coroners in Florida. The counties that contain a large city may have only that one county in the district, but in more rural areas, multiple counties comprise a district.

Georgia (mixed). In Georgia, 154 of the 159 counties have elected coroners who need not be physicians. These coroners rely on state-appointed medical examiners in various locations around the state to conduct autopsies when needed. Five counties in the Atlanta area (Fulton, DeKalb, Cobb, Gwinnett, and Clayton) have abolished the office of coroner and each has a medical examiner system. A state medical examiner has been created to oversee regional medical examiner and coroner activities in Georgia for those counties that still have coroners. There are state-funded autopsy facilities in Augusta, Macon, Savannah, Moultrie, Atlanta, and Summerville (Trion), autopsy services are regionalized, and each facility serves coroners in multiple counties. Four counties with a county medical examiner each have their own medical examiner's office and morgue, while the fifth (Clayton) uses the autopsy facility at the GBI Crime Lab in Atlanta.

Hawaii (mixed). The city and county of Honolulu are served by a medical examiner who is appointed, must be board certified in anatomic or forensic pathology, and who serves as *ex officio* coroner. The county chief of police, who is elected in the counties of Hawaii, Maui, Kalawao, and Kauai, serves as *ex officio* coroner. The coroners rely upon appointed coroner physicians to perform autopsies and examine bodies, who must also be board certified in anatomic or forensic pathology.

Idaho (coroner). The 44 counties in Idaho are each served by elected coroners who need not be physicians. They rely on local pathologists and other physicians to perform autopsies and examine bodies.

Illinois (mixed). Most of the 102 counties in Illinois are served by elected or appointed coroners who need not be a physician. They rely on pathologists and other physicians to examine bodies and perform autopsies. Cook County (Chicago) is served by an appointed medical examiner who must be a board certified pathologist. In a few counties, the elected sheriff serves as the coroner.

Indiana (mixed). The 92 counties in Indiana are each served by an elected county coroner who need not be a physician. To perform autopsies, they rely upon medical examiners who are appointed and who must be board certified anatomic pathologists.

Iowa (ME). The 99 counties in Iowa are served by an appointed state medical examiner who must have special knowledge in forensic pathology. In addition, each county has a county-appointed medical examiner who must be a physician. Many death investigations are done locally, with reports being sent to the state office. There are no coroners in Iowa.

Kansas (coroner). Kansas is somewhat unique in that its 105 counties are served by 31 appointed, district coroners who serve multiple counties and who must be physicians. Pathologists are relied upon as needed to perform autopsies and examine bodies.

Kentucky (mixed). Each of the 120 counties in Kentucky is served by an elected coroner who need not be a physician. Throughout the state, there are medical examiners (who must be board certified forensic pathologists) and district medical examiners (who must be pathologists), who provide autopsy services. Further, there is a state-appointed state medical examiner who oversees coroner, medical examiner, and district medical examiner activities in the state. The system is organized throughout the Kentucky Justice Cabinet based in Frankfurt. The state medical examiner is based in Louisville. Medical examiners and district medical examiners are located in other larger cities in the state.

Louisiana (coroner). Each of the 64 parishes (counties) in Louisiana is served by an elected coroner who must be a physician (unless no physician will serve). They rely on pathologists and forensic pathologists around the state to conduct bodily examinations and autopsies. There is no statewide organization.

Maine (ME). The 16 counties in Maine are served by an appointed state chief medical examiner who serves in Augusta, and who must be board certified or show proficiency in forensic pathology. The chief medical examiner may appoint other physicians and pathologists to serve as medical examiners or deputy medical examiners. There are no coroners in Maine.

Maryland (ME). The 23 counties and the city of Baltimore are served by an appointed state chief medical examiner who must have training in pathology. The Postmortem Examiners Commission appoints the chief and deputy chief medical examiners, and assistant medical examiners. It also appoints a physician in each county to serve as the deputy medical examiners. Information from each death is reported to the state office, but some death investigations are conducted locally. There are no coroners in Maryland.

Massachusetts (ME). The 14 counties in Massachusetts are served by a state-appointed state chief medical examiner who must be a board certified forensic pathologist. The chief is located in Boston and oversees regions served by physician medical examiners. The regions consist of groups of counties, within which there may be multiple district medical examiners. Death investigations are conducted locally (not all in the state office), with some information for each case being reported to the state office. There are no coroners in Massachusetts.

Michigan (ME). Each of the 83 counties in Michigan is served by an appointed medical examiner, who must be a physician. These medical examiners rely upon pathologists (or forensic pathologists) to perform autopsies. There are no coroners in Michigan. Death investigations are not organized on a statewide level, and each county operates somewhat autonomously.

Minnesota (mixed). Most of the 87 counties in Minnesota are served by elected or appointed coroners (depending on the county's method of choice) who need not be physicians, but about 13 counties are served by appointed medical examiners who must be physicians, including the two large counties in Minneapolis-St. Paul. The system is not organized on a statewide basis, and each system runs somewhat autonomously. Nonphysician coroners rely on available anatomic or forensic pathologists to perform autopsies when needed.

Mississippi (ME). The 82 counties in Mississippi are served by an appointed state medical examiner, who must be board certified in forensic pathology, and who is based in Jackson. Each county has either an elected county medical examiner who must be a physician, or an elected county medical examiner investigator who need not be a physician. The state medical examiner oversees death investigation activities in the state. The county medical examiners rely on the state medical examiner or other anatomic or forensic pathologists to perform autopsies, when needed. Although the county medical examiner investigators function somewhat as coroners, they are not officially titled as coroners.

Missouri (mixed). The 115 counties are served mostly by elected coroners who need not be physicians, while 10 counties are served by appointed medical examiners who must be physicians. Coroners rely on anatomic or forensic pathologists to perform autopsies for them when needed. As is the usual case, the smaller and rural counties tend to have coroners while the cities and larger counties tend to have medical examiners.

Montana (mixed). The 56 counties in Montana are each served by an elected coroner, who need not be a physician. In addition, there is a state-appointed chief state medical examiner who must be a forensic pathologist and certified by the American Board of Pathology. The chief state medical examiner oversees physician associate medical examiners who are located in several places in the state to provide autopsy services for the county coroners.

Nebraska (coroner). Each of the 93 counties in Nebraska is served by an elected county attorney who serves as ex officio coroner, and who may delegate to the elected county sheriff those duties that relate to the viewing of dead bodies. Coroners may appoint physicians to serve as coroner's physicians to provide autopsy services and otherwise assist the coroner in carrying out the duties of the office.

Nevada (coroner). Each of the 17 counties in Nevada is served by a coroner. In most counties the elected sheriff serves as ex officio coroner, but other counties appoint a coroner and determine their own requirements for serving as coroner. Clark County (Las Vegas) also has a medical examiner to assist the coroner. In other areas of the state, the coroners rely on autopsy or forensic pathologists to conduct examinations of bodies.

New Hampshire (ME). The 10 counties in New Hampshire are served by an appointed state medical examiner based in Concord, who must be a board certified pathologist with special competence in forensic pathology. The state medical examiner is assisted by county medical examiners who must be physicians.

New Jersey (ME). The 21 counties in New Jersey are served by an appointed state medical examiner who must be a qualified forensic pathologist, and who is based in Newark. Appointed county medical examiners also conduct investigations and file reports with the state office. Counties may jointly appoint an intercounty medical examiner to serve a region of the state.

New Mexico (ME). The state medical investigator must be a physician, preferably trained in pathology and forensic pathology, and is appointed by the Board of Medical Investigators. The state medical examiner is based in Albuquerque at the University of New Mexico School of Medicine, and autopsies are performed there on bodies transported from throughout the 33 counties in the state. District medical investigators are physicians appointed by the state medical investigator to assist locally with death investigations. The pathologists at the Office of the Medical Investigator at Albuquerque also perform institution-based death investigations on patients who die at the university hospital. It is difficult for the state medical investigator to visit scenes personally because of the large area covered by the office (the whole state), so he or she must rely on information supplied by local authorities and the district medical investigators.

New York (mixed). Most of the 62 counties have more than one elected county coroner (usually two) who need not be physicians, and each has equal authority. They rely on physicians called county coroner's physicians to assist with death investigations and autopsies. Some counties, such as those that include New York City and most of the larger cities, have abolished the office of coroner and have a county medical examiner who is appointed by county authorities and must be a physician.

North Carolina (ME). The 100 counties in North Carolina are served by a state chief medical examiner, based in Chapel Hill, who is appointed by the state government and who must be a board certified forensic pathologist. The state medical examiner may appoint county medical examiners who may or may not be physicians, and who can assist with death investigations. Most of the larger cities have medical examiners who conduct autopsies locally (such as Winston-Salem), but information is filed at the state medical examiner's office. Some medical examiners who are not physicians or pathologists function like death investigators and collect information, but they rely on other medical examiners or pathologists to perform autopsies.

North Dakota (coroner). Each of the 53 counties in North Dakota is served by a county-appointed coroner who, in counties of more than 8,000 people, must be a physician. Some coroners (if a pathologist or physician) may perform autopsies or they rely on other pathologists to perform autopsies when needed.

Ohio (mixed). Each of the 88 counties in Ohio has an elected coroner (except Summit County, which has a medical examiner) who must be a physician. Each may appoint other physicians to serve as chief deputy coroner. Most coroners, although physicians, do not actually perform the autopsies, but rely on pathologists to do so.

Oklahoma (ME). The 77 counties are served by a state chief medical examiner, based in Oklahoma City, and appointed by the Board of Medicolegal Investigations. The state chief medical examiner works with county medical examiners who serve at the pleasure of the state chief medical examiner, and assist locally with death investigations throughout the state. Some death investigations and autopsies are performed locally, but information is filed at the state chief medical examiner's office.

Oregon (ME). The 36 counties in Oregon are served by a state medical examiner, now based in Portland, who must be a physician and pathologist, and who is appointed by state authorities and an advisory board. The state medical examiner, in conjunction with county authorities, may appoint district medical examiners who must be physicians, and who can conduct death investigations in various parts of the state. Information from local death investigations is filed with the state medical examiner's office.

Pennsylvania (mixed). Each of the 67 counties (except Philadelphia and Allegheny County [Pittsburgh]) has an elected coroner who need not be a physician. Coroners rely on pathologists to perform autopsies when needed. Philadelphia has an appointed medical examiner who is a forensic pathologist.

Rhode Island (ME). The 5 counties are served by a chief medical examiner, appointed by the governor with advice from the State Medical Commission, and who must be certified in anatomic pathology with training or experience in forensic pathology. The chief medical examiner is based in Providence and conducts death investigations for all areas of the state.

South Carolina (mixed). Although counties with populations of 100,000 or more may choose to have a medical examiner system, every county has a coroner who is elected and who need not be a physician. In Charleston and Greenville there are also medical examiners who are appointed by county authorities and who work with the coroner to provide autopsy and death investigation services. Other county coroners rely upon available physicians or pathologists to perform autopsies.

South Dakota (coroner). Each of the 66 counties is served by an elected coroner who need not be a physician. Coroners rely upon physicians and pathologists to perform autopsies when needed.

Tennessee (ME). The 95 counties are served by a medical examiner system. The state chief medical examiner is appointed by the governor and state authorities, must be a physician with special interest or training in forensic pathology, and oversees medicolegal death investigation activities in the state. Many counties have a county medical examiner who is elected by the local county governing body and who must be a physician. County medical examiners conduct death investigations locally. Usually, one of the county medical examiners is appointed as the state chief medical examiner, who is presently based in Nashville and serves as the county medical examiner for Davidson County.

Texas (Mixed). Most of the 254 counties have multiple justices of the peace who are elected, need not be physicians, and who serve as coroner. Some of the counties with larger cities such as Dallas, Fort Worth, San Antonio, Corpus Christi, Houston,

El Paso, Galveston, and several others, have a medical examiner who is appointed by county authorities.

Utah (ME). The 29 counties in Utah are served by a state-appointed state medical examiner who must be board certified in forensic pathology and who is based in Salt Lake City. All death investigations in the state are conducted through the state medical examiner's office.

Vermont (ME). The 14 counties are served by a chief medical examiner who is appointed by the state board of health, and for whom there are no specific statutory requirements. Regional Medical Examiners must be physicians and are appointed by the chief medical examiner. The chief medical examiner's office is based in Burlington.

Virginia (ME). The 95 counties and 41 independent cities are served by a chief medical examiner appointed by state authorities, who oversees medicolegal death investigation in the state (commonwealth). The chief medical examiner appoints various county and city medical examiners, who must be physicians and who conduct death investigations locally. Currently, the chief medical examiner is based in Richmond. There are also assistant chief medical examiners, appointed by the chief medical examiner, who must be forensic pathologists who can perform autopsies in various districts of the state.

Washington (mixed). Most of the 39 counties are served by coroners who are specifically elected as the coroner in some counties, while in other counties the elected prosecuting attorney serves as ex officio coroner. King County (Seattle) and Snohomish County (Everett) have appointed county medical examiners. The counties with coroners rely on pathologists to perform autopsies. In Washington, the coroner may not be the owner or an employee of a funeral home or mortuary.

West Virginia (ME). The 55 counties are served by a chief medical examiner who is appointed by the state director of health and must be a physician who is eligible for certification in pathology. The chief may appoint county medical examiners who need not be physicians but usually have a paramedical or other related background. Death investigations are conducted locally in some areas such as Morgantown. The state chief medical examiner oversees death investigation activities for the state.

Wisconsin (mixed). Most of the 72 counties have an elected coroner who need not be a physician. Some counties do not have a coroner, but have an appointed medical examiner who need not be a physician and who is appointed by the County Board of Supervisors. Other counties, such as Milwaukee, have an appointed medical examiner who, by county regulation, is required to be a physician or pathologist.

Wyoming (coroner). Each of the 23 counties have an elected coroner who need not be a physician. They rely upon physicians or pathologists to perform autopsies.

A few broad, sweeping generalizations may be made. ME states tend to be concentrated in the northeastern United States and mid-Atlantic states. Coroner states tend to be those with large rural areas. Mixed states are the most common type. Most states have a state association of coroners or medical examiners (depending on the state) for the purpose of facilitating communication, education, and political goals in the state. You may be able to obtain further information from such organizations about the people and activities in your state relevant to death investigation.

For additional information, see http://www.cdc.gov/epo/dphsi/mecisp/index.htm and for links to specific organizations and coroner's or medical examiner's offices, see http://www.fcmeo/org/COMECA.htm

Part VI

Special Circumstances

24 What about Mass Fatality Incidents?

Imagine that you are the coroner of a small rural county and the sheriff calls and tells you that a commercial airliner has just crashed in your county and it suspected that all 256 people on board are dead. What on earth do you do? Not only have you never been involved in such a situation, but even if you had been, the amount of work involved to investigate and manage such a mass disaster is too much for one or two people to handle. Further, the county morgue can only hold five bodies at a time.

Fortunately, there are many sources of assistance available. Most counties and states have a *disaster plan* that has been developed to project responses in advance for such disaster situations. There is usually a disaster coordinator who is in charge of managing emergency responses and transport of dead bodies. The local coordinator may call on state or federal assistance if needed. Arrangements have usually been made to borrow or rent refrigerated trucks to store remains until they can be processed and examined, and to obtain body bags so remains can be kept separate from one another. There are usually other coroners or medical examiners in the state who will volunteer or who may be called upon to assist in the processing and examination of the bodies.

There are a number of federal government agencies and programs that may be called upon as well. For example, the D-MAT team (disaster medical assistance team) is available to provide medical services for the injured, and a D-MORT (disaster mortuary operations and recovery team) is available to assist with the management of dead bodies. For example, after severe flooding in south Georgia caused more than 200 coffins to be washed out of the ground, the D-MORT team assisted with recovery and identification of the remains so they could be properly reinterred. They also assist in acute disaster situations such as Hurricane Katrina, in which the bodies of many deceased persons needed to be recovered and processed. The Armed Forces Medical Examiner System also has a special team designed to assist in the identification of remains, and can provide medical examiner services as well to assist with examination of dead bodies.

Depending on the type of the disaster, there may be a specific agency that is given authority to investigate. For example, in all commercial airline crashes, the National Transportation Safety Board (NTSB) investigates the crash to determine whether the crash was due to pilot error, equipment failure, or external factors such as weather. The Federal Aviation Administration has a toxicology laboratory to which specimens from the pilots in airplane crashes may be sent for testing. In bombings, the FBI's Bureau of Alcohol, Tobacco, and Firearms investigates the bomb scene to identify the nature of the bomb and to find its source. Usually, however, no matter what agency investigates the disaster scene, the medicolegal part of the death investigation (determining the cause, manner, and circumstances of death) is conducted by the coroner or medical examiner who would normally have had jurisdiction in the area. Of course, cooperation between the medical examiner or coroner and the other investigative agencies is essential for smooth and adequate investigation to occur. Many of the agencies designed to respond to disasters only assist if they are asked to do so. In some instances, however, such as commercial airline crashes, federal law requires investigation by a specific agency. In recent years, federal involvement has intensified through the Department of Homeland Security and the FBI, which become involved in terrorist and other attacks, such as those using biological or chemical weapons.

Some of the more common types of mass fatalities that involve medical examiners and coroners in the United States are airplane crashes, bus crashes, fires, and mining disasters.

The extent of a mass fatality incident can vary considerably from involving only a few dead people to hundreds or thousands at a time. Some people define a mass disaster as any incident in which four or more people are killed in the same incident. Thus, the resources needed to manage a mass fatality incident vary considerably depending on the type and extent of the disaster. The two most extensive mass fatality incidents in recent years were the World Trade Center terrorist attack and the Tsunami devastation in the Pacific.

25 Deaths on Indian Reservations or Federal Property

Native American (Indian) reservations operate under their own laws, and in general do not fall under the jurisdiction of the medical examiner or coroner who serves the adjacent lands. The federal government has a Bureau of Indian Affairs and an Indian Health Service through which some death investigation activities may be organized. In many areas the reservations have made arrangements with a local medical examiner or coroner to conduct death investigations when needed.

Similarly, when a death occurs in a federal building, on other federal property, in a federal prison, or on a military base, the local medical examiner or coroner does not have jurisdiction to investigate the death. In such cases the federal government may call upon its own resources to conduct such investigations, using the staff of agencies such as the Armed Forces Medical Examiner who has personnel stationed at various places in the country and throughout the world. More often than not, however, the local federal authorities will have made arrangements for the local medical examiner or coroner to conduct such investigations, or they will have a contract with a local autopsy physician or forensic pathologist to perform autopsies.

When a civilian dies on a military base or federal property the local medical examiner or coroner is usually given jurisdiction in the case. The same holds true when a military person or federal worker or employee dies outside of federal or military property. Some exceptions include the death of the President or Vice President of the United States, and the death of pilots who are operating military aircraft that crash on nonfederal property.

Part VII

Other Death Investigation Topics

26 Who May Give Permission for an Autopsy?

As mentioned earlier, the laws in each state usually describe who may give permission for institution-based and privately arranged autopsies, and which relatives or next of kin are given preference over other relatives or next of kin with respect to permissions (Figure 26.1). Although state laws vary, usually they adhere to the following general scheme:

- Top priority is usually given to a person who has power of attorney over the deceased's affairs. This may be a relative or other person.
- In the absence of a power of attorney, the person's spouse is the one who must give permission for autopsy. In many states, a common-law spouse may do this if there has not been an official marriage, although the definition of common-law spouse varies among states.
- If there is no spouse, then an adult son or daughter of the decedent may give permission. If one such person gives permission and the others object, the permission of one is usually considered adequate.
- If there are no adult sons or daughters, then an adult sibling such as a brother or sister may give permission. If there are no siblings, then another adult relative such as an aunt or uncle may give permission.
- In some circumstances, there may be no remaining family members to give permission. In such cases, the person who takes charge of the body for burial is allowed to determine whether or not autopsy permission is granted. In some instances the county or state may have to assume custody of the body for burial. In such cases, the Department of Family and Children Services or another agency at the county or state level that takes custody of the body for burial can assign permission for autopsy.
- It is acceptable for a person to stipulate in a will the desire that his or her body be autopsied after death. This sometimes poses a tricky problem because upon death, the body becomes the property of the next of kin. It is an interesting legal question as to whether a person's expressed desire for autopsy should outweigh the next of kin's rights after death. Much of the legal community feels that the decedent's wishes should outweigh those of the next of kin, but others feel that the next of kin should be allowed to decide regardless of what the person expressed prior to death. At present this interesting problem may be handled differently in different

Who Gives Permission for Institution-based Autopsies?

- The person having Power of Attorney for the decedent's affairs
- The decedent's spouse
- An adult son or daughter of the decedent
- A brother or sister of the decedent
- Another relative of the decedent
- The person or agency accepting responsibility and custody of the body for burial or cremation

NOTE: The highest one on this list, existing in a given case, is required

FIGURE 26.1   When an autopsy is done at a hospital and not under the authority of a medical examiner or coroner, permission must be obtained to perform the autopsy. In a given case, it must be established which living relatives or family members exist, and the highest one on the list is the one who must give permission for autopsy. If there is more than one person of equal rank (such as a brother and a sister), the permission of one of them is usually sufficient.

states. The best way to avoid such problems is to discuss autopsy with family members prior to death, so that all interested parties know what is desired and what is expected. This may include a statement in the will that an autopsy is desired and an indication of whom should give permission for autopsy upon the death of the subject.

- Of course, if a death falls under the provisions of the law that require a medicolegal death investigation, then the family may have no say as to whether an autopsy is performed. If you become involved in a death for which medicolegal autopsy may occur by law, but you feel adamantly that an autopsy need not or should not be performed, it is acceptable to call the medical examiner and coroner and let them know your feelings. Most medical examiners and coroners will take the family's requests seriously and will not perform an autopsy if the important questions that have arisen can be answered without autopsy. However, on many occasions it is necessary to perform an autopsy to fulfill the requirements of the law and the ultimate decision may not be what the family desires.
- In a private death investigation, whoever the family or their attorney contacts to perform the investigation or autopsy will probably require written permission from the family, much in the same fashion that is required for institution-based death investigation and autopsy.

27 The Autopsy Report

The way in which autopsy findings are reported depends on the pathologist, the institution, and the type and needs of the case in question. Although some guidelines exist on recommended ways of preparing autopsy reports, there is no method that is universally used by everyone who performs autopsies. Further, autopsy reports for institution-based death investigations tend to differ slightly from those in medicolegal death investigations in that the former tend to be a little longer, more medically oriented in terminology, and somewhat excessive in detail. Regardless of how the autopsy is reported, the report tends to contain the following types of information.

Reason for performing the examination. There is usually at least a brief statement that indicates why the autopsy or examination is being performed. For example: "This 47 year-old white male collapsed while working and did not have a history of medical problems. An autopsy is performed to determine the cause and manner of death." In institution-based autopsies, there is often a lengthy summary of the patient's course while in the institution (i.e., a review and summary of the medical record).

Date, time, and place of examination; attendees. For documentation purposes, the report usually includes the type of information as in this statement: "Under the provisions of the State Death Investigation Act, a complete autopsy is performed at the county morgue on Friday, November 10, 1995, commencing at 8:15 AM with the assistance of Robert Good. In attendance are Detectives Mike Smith and George Blount of the County Police Department."

Presentation, clothing, personal effects, and evidence. There is usually some description of how the body was wrapped (i.e., in a white sheet) or enclosed (i.e., in a black body bag), as well as an inventory and description of clothing, jewelry, other personal effects, and other items with the body that might constitute evidence.

Postmortem imaging studies. A statement is usually included indicating whether or not postmortem x-rays were performed, and if so, the findings.

Postmortem changes. Characteristic findings that occur after death as the body goes through its decomposition changes are usually described. These include the presence or absence of stiffening (rigor mortis), the distribution and intensity of blood that settles in the tissues (livor mortis), the degree of clouding and collapse of the corneas (clear part of the eye), discolorations in or slippage of the skin, and other potential postmortem changes. These findings are often used to evaluate the position the body may have been in after death occurred, or to get a rough estimate of the time that has elapsed since death.

Diagnostic and therapeutic artifacts. Usually there is a description of any needle marks, intravenous tubing, tubes in the nose and mouth, incisions, and other findings that may have been created by medical personnel who were trying to resuscitate or treat the deceased. It is important to identify such findings so they are not confused with injuries that may have been inflicted by someone who assaulted, battered, or otherwise injured the deceased.

Features of identification. The deceased's height, weight, hair color (including length and texture), visible scars and tattoos, visibly missing body parts (such as amputations), condition of the teeth, and other distinctive features are usually documented. Occasionally the real identity of a person will be questioned after autopsy, and information that may help confirm identity is helpful. The information may also assist in interpretations of evidence found at scenes (such as hair), or in reconstructions of events such as shootings, in which case the deceased's physical characteristics, such as height, might help determine the location from which a gunshot could have been fired.

External examination of the body. This involves a thorough examination of all parts of the body externally, including the head, face, and scalp; the neck; the chest, abdomen, and back; the groin; the genitalia; the anus, rectum, and the area around the anus (perineum); the upper extremities (shoulders, arms, forearms, wrists, and hands); and the lower extremities (hips, thighs, knees, legs, ankles, and feet). Not only are observed findings documented, but quite often the absence of certain findings is also documented in the report. For example, the report might state: "There is no evidence of abrasion, contusion, or other marks on the neck."

Internal examination of the body. This usually involves a thorough description of the inner aspects of the body, including the internal organs and tissues, and is often regionalized into the head, neck, chest, abdomen, and pelvis. There are usually specific descriptions of the heart and circulatory system, the nervous system, the respiratory system (lungs and airways), the endocrine system (thyroid, adrenal gland), the reticuloendothelial system (spleen, lymph nodes, bone marrow), the digestive system (esophagus, stomach, small and large intestines, liver, pancreas, and gallbladder), the musculoskeletal system (bone and muscle), and the soft tissue (subcutaneous parts of the skin and underlying fat). There is often mention of whether unusual color changes or odors are perceived, which may occasionally be seen in some types of drug and poison cases.

Other procedures. There is usually a listing of the procedures, samples taken, and other tests that are performed such as photographs, fingerprints, hand wipings for gunshot residue, tissue for histologic examination, blood and urine for toxicology, vitreous fluid from the eye for chemical tests, and many other possibilities.

Preliminary findings. After the gross portion of the examination (gross is a medical term for *macroscopic* or visible with the naked eye), a listing of findings and diagnoses is usually stated summarizing the findings in the case as of the time the autopsy dissection is completed.

Results. After results of various tests become available, results of relevant tests are often included in the autopsy report to eliminate the need to refer to multiple documents and to enable the autopsy report to tell the whole story.

Final diagnoses and findings. This section includes a listing of the diagnoses and findings after all available information has been considered. Although it is often referred to as "final," if additional information becomes available, the "final" findings may be changed or updated.

Cause, manner, and circumstances of death. The report usually contains a statement regarding the cause of death (e.g., gunshot wound of the head), the manner of death (e.g., homicide), and a description of how the injury occurred (e.g., shot by another person).

Comment/Opinion. Many pathologists include a comment that is directed at answering predictable questions or to explain findings that might be confusing. For example, in a gunshot wound case the comment might be: "The findings indicate that the gunshot wound is a tight contact wound with the gun having been pressed tightly on the skin when fired. The angle of the wound track is front to back and upward at a 30 degree angle with no lateral deviation. Because the bullet exited, no projectile was recovered. The findings are consistent with the reported information that the wound was self-inflicted." A sample autopsy report is included in Chapter 41.

In medicolegal death investigations, there is usually an *Evidence of Injury* section of the autopsy report in which external and internal injuries are described and correlated.

28 The Death Certificate

Each state (and the District of Columbia) has an official death certificate that serves several purposes:

1. *Documentation of the fact of death*: That is, that a specific person died at a specified place, date, and time. If the person cannot be identified, the death certificate is usually filed under a name such as John Doe #6, or Jane Doe #4.
2. *Clarification of the cause and circumstances of death*: This includes several items. One is the cause of death (i.e., what actually caused the person to die, such as a gunshot wound of the head). Another is the manner of death, which is a classification of the type of circumstance under which the death occurred. If death is due solely to disease or aging, the manner of death is natural. If death resulted from an unintentional injury, the manner is *accident*. If death came about because of an intentional injury, then the manner of death is *homicide* if the injury was inflicted by another person or *suicide* if the injury was intentionally inflicted by the deceased. When the manner of death cannot be determined, it is usually stated as "undetermined," "could not be determined," or "unclassified." For the purpose of determining the manner of death, poisonings are managed in the same way as injuries because injuries and poisonings constitute *external causes*. There is also a place to indicate specifically how an injury occurred (such as "electrocuted by high voltage power line"), and the date, time, and place that it occurred.
3. *Information about the deceased*: This includes information such as the deceased's age, race, date of birth, place of residence at the time of death, birthplace, and other descriptive information.
4. *Information about disposition of the remains*: This information usually indicates the funeral director's name and information about where the body was buried or otherwise disposed of, such as being buried, cremated, or buried at sea.

Each state's death certificate is based on a U.S. Standard Certificate of Death. However, each state's death certificate differs in some way from all the other states. Such variations may include the size of the death certificate form, the number of copies, the items of information that are included on the form, and other variations. The section that includes the cause, manner, and circumstances of death is similar in each state, but minor variations occur such as the number of lines provided to write the cause of death. The U.S. Standard Certificate of Death is based on recommendations of the World Health Organization (WHO), and because the U.S. is a signatory to WHO agreements, it generally follows the WHO recommendations.

Most portions of the death certificate are usually completed by the funeral director, except for the cause of death section, which is completed and certified by a physician, medical examiner, or coroner. A patient's private physician signs the death certificate when death is due to natural causes and the medical examiner or coroner need not be notified, or when the medical examiner or coroner has been notified but declines to investigate the death. If death was brought about or hastened by an injury or poisoning of any type, the medical examiner or coroner will usually sign the death certificate. This is done to help ensure that deaths from external causes (injury and poisoning) have the opportunity to be consistently investigated and certified as to the cause, manner, and circumstances of death.

Most states require that a death certificate be filed within a few days to a week or so of death. However, because the information needed to certify the death may not be available within that time period, most states allow a death certificate to be filed as "pending further information." The death certificate is then amended (updated) at a later time when the information becomes available. Most states also have some policy concerning how long a case may be held as pending, which may extend for several weeks or months depending on the state.

Once the physician, medical examiner, or coroner completes his or her part of the death certificate and the funeral director completes his or her parts, the funeral director generally files the death certificate with a county or state registrar in charge of keeping death certificates (plus birth certificates and other records) on behalf of the state. The funeral director will usually provide a few certified copies of the death certificate to the family once the death certificate has been filed with the registrar. Certified copies may also be obtained directly from the registrar's office (often at the county or state health department) for a nominal fee of a few dollars.

Although the death certificate is often used as a legal document to prove the fact of death, it is not written in stone and information can be changed if errors are discovered. Usually, the person who completed the original death certificate must request that such changes be made, and do so in writing.

Information from the death certificate is coded using a system called the International Classification of Diseases (ICD), in which numbers are applied to the diagnoses or conditions on the death certificate. The ICD system is used in many places in the world, and is also based on recommendations of the WHO (World Health Organization). Persons called nosologists review the death certificate and apply the numerical codes. Many counties keep files of the data as do the states. In turn, the data are sent to the National Center for Health Statistics so that nationwide mortality data can be assembled. The federal government, through the National Center for Health Statistics, pays the states for this information to foster compliance with submitting the data in a standard format. Usually the national data lag behind by about two years. That is, in 2005 the most recent national data available for general use are for the year 2003.

Politicians, government agencies, and researchers use cause-of-death information when they make decisions about which health programs to prioritize and fund. It is important that cause-of-death statistics be accurate.

Death certificates are usually officially filed with the registrar in the county *where death occurred*, which often differs from the county where the deceased lived or the county in which the injury or events leading to death occurred. It is not uncommon, however, for a courtesy copy of the death certificate to be forwarded to the county where the decedent lived so accurate statistics can be kept in that county as well. The same applies to visitors who die somewhere other than their home state — a copy of the death certificate may be sent to the deceased's home state. Records are shared so that birth certificates and death certificates may ultimately be matched up to document the life course of a specific person, and as a quality control procedure to assure accurate record keeping concerning vital statistics (i.e., birth, marriage, and death certificates), and to ensure that there is ultimately a death certificate that can be matched with a birth certificate.

Remember that many medical examiners and coroners are required to investigate cases in which a fatal injury occurred in their county, even when death actually occurred in another county. This creates the possibility that a person who lives in one county may be injured in another county and die in a third county. Thus, multiple counties may be involved in processing records that relate to a specific death.

Unfortunately, many physicians, medical examiners, and coroners do a substandard job of completing their part of the death certificate. The information is often incomplete, vaguely stated, and sometimes inaccurate. A major reason for this problem is that few physicians receive official training on how to complete a death certificate, and most physicians sign few if any death certificates, so they lack experience in doing so. Efforts are underway to address these problems, such as providing educational materials and system changes that enable more complete, accurate, and consistent information to appear on death certificates. In the near future, web-based computer programs will probably be used to assist in these goals.

Remember that the cause and manner stated on the death certificate represent the *opinion* of the certifier, and may or may not be correct. The certifier's opinion is stated to the best of the certifier's knowledge, and need be based only on reasonable medical probability (i.e., more likely than not). Some states, however, in reference to suicide, have laws that require the evidence for suicide to constitute a preponderance of evidence, which is more than just a 51% certainty level.

The death certificate contains limited information. To fully evaluate the circumstances and details of a specific death, it may be necessary to review other documents and records such as police reports, death investigation reports, autopsy reports, and crime lab reports.

Overall, the death certificate documents the facts and basic circumstances of death and is used for legal, administrative, and statistical purposes.

The current (2003) version of the United States Standard Certificate of Death, a model on which the death certificate of each state is based, along with examples of completed cause of death sections of the death certificate, are shown in Figure 28.1 and Figure 28.2.

For further information about mortality statistics, see www.cdc.gov/nchs.

U.S. STANDARD CERTIFICATE OF DEATH

LOCAL FILE NO. _____   STATE FILE NO. _____

1. DECEDENT'S LEGAL NAME (Include AKA's if any) (First, Middle, Last)	2. SEX 3. SOCIAL SECURITY NUMBER

4a. AGE-Last Birthday (Years)	4b. UNDER 1 YEAR	4c. UNDER 1 DAY	5. DATE OF BIRTH (Mo/Day/Yr)	6. BIRTHPLACE (City and State or Foreign Country)
	Months Days	Hours Minutes		

7a. RESIDENCE-STATE	7b. COUNTY	7c. CITY OR TOWN

7d. STREET AND NUMBER	7e. APT. NO.	7f. ZIP CODE	7g. INSIDE CITY LIMITS? ☐ Yes ☐ No

8. EVER IN US ARMED FORCES? ☐ Yes ☐ No	9. MARITAL STATUS AT TIME OF DEATH ☐ Married ☐ Married, but separated ☐ Widowed ☐ Divorced ☐ Never Married ☐ Unknown	10. SURVIVING SPOUSE'S NAME (If wife, give name prior to first marriage)

11. FATHER'S NAME (First, Middle, Last)	12. MOTHER'S NAME PRIOR TO FIRST MARRIAGE (First, Middle, Last)

13a. INFORMANT'S NAME	13b. RELATIONSHIP TO DECEDENT	13c. MAILING ADDRESS (Street and Number, City, State, Zip Code)

14. PLACE OF DEATH (Check only one: see instructions)

IF DEATH OCCURRED IN A HOSPITAL: ☐ Inpatient ☐ Emergency Room/Outpatient ☐ Dead on Arrival	IF DEATH OCCURRED SOMEWHERE OTHER THAN A HOSPITAL: ☐ Hospice facility ☐ Nursing home/Long term care facility ☐ Decedent's home ☐ Other (Specify):

15. FACILITY NAME (If not institution, give street & number)	16. CITY OR TOWN , STATE, AND ZIP CODE	17. COUNTY OF DEATH

18. METHOD OF DISPOSITION: ☐ Burial ☐ Cremation ☐ Donation ☐ Entombment ☐ Removal from State ☐ Other (Specify):	19. PLACE OF DISPOSITION (Name of cemetery, crematory, other place)

20. LOCATION-CITY, TOWN, AND STATE	21. NAME AND COMPLETE ADDRESS OF FUNERAL FACILITY

22. SIGNATURE OF FUNERAL SERVICE LICENSEE OR OTHER AGENT	23. LICENSE NUMBER (Of Licensee)

ITEMS 24-28 MUST BE COMPLETED BY PERSON WHO PRONOUNCES OR CERTIFIES DEATH	24. DATE PRONOUNCED DEAD (Mo/Day/Yr)	25. TIME PRONOUNCED DEAD

26. SIGNATURE OF PERSON PRONOUNCING DEATH (Only when applicable)	27. LICENSE NUMBER	28. DATE SIGNED (Mo/Day/Yr)

29. ACTUAL OR PRESUMED DATE OF DEATH (Mo/Day/Yr) (Spell Month)	30. ACTUAL OR PRESUMED TIME OF DEATH	31. WAS MEDICAL EXAMINER OR CORONER CONTACTED? ☐ Yes ☐ No

CAUSE OF DEATH (See instructions and examples)

32. PART I. Enter the chain of events—diseases, injuries, or complications—that directly caused the death. DO NOT enter terminal events such as cardiac arrest, respiratory arrest, or ventricular fibrillation without showing the etiology. DO NOT ABBREVIATE. Enter only one cause on a line. Add additional lines if necessary.

Approximate interval: Onset to death

IMMEDIATE CAUSE (Final disease or condition resulting in death) ----→ a. _____
Due to (or as a consequence of):

Sequentially list conditions, if any, leading to the cause listed on line a. Enter the UNDERLYING CAUSE (disease or injury that initiated the events resulting in death) LAST
b. _____
Due to (or as a consequence of):

c. _____
Due to (or as a consequence of):

d. _____

PART II. Enter other significant conditions contributing to death but not resulting in the underlying cause given in PART I

33. WAS AN AUTOPSY PERFORMED? ☐ Yes ☐ No
34. WERE AUTOPSY FINDINGS AVAILABLE TO COMPLETE THE CAUSE OF DEATH? ☐ Yes ☐ No

35. DID TOBACCO USE CONTRIBUTE TO DEATH? ☐ Yes ☐ Probably ☐ No ☐ Unknown	36. IF FEMALE: ☐ Not pregnant within past year ☐ Pregnant at time of death ☐ Not pregnant, but pregnant within 42 days of death ☐ Not pregnant, but pregnant 43 days to 1 year before death ☐ Unknown if pregnant within the past year	37. MANNER OF DEATH ☐ Natural ☐ Homicide ☐ Accident ☐ Pending Investigation ☐ Suicide ☐ Could not be determined

38. DATE OF INJURY (Mo/Day/Yr) (Spell Month)	39. TIME OF INJURY	40. PLACE OF INJURY (e.g., Decedent's home; construction site; restaurant; wooded area)	41. INJURY AT WORK? ☐ Yes ☐ No

42. LOCATION OF INJURY: State: City or Town:

Street & Number: Apartment No.:   Zip Code:

43. DESCRIBE HOW INJURY OCCURRED:	44. IF TRANSPORTATION INJURY, SPECIFY: ☐ Driver/Operator ☐ Passenger ☐ Pedestrian ☐ Other (Specify)

45. CERTIFIER (Check only one):
☐ Certifying physician-To the best of my knowledge, death occurred due to the cause(s) and manner stated.
☐ Pronouncing & Certifying physician-To the best of my knowledge, death occurred at the time, date, and place, and due to the cause(s) and manner stated.
☐ Medical Examiner/Coroner-On the basis of examination, and/or investigation, in my opinion, death occurred at the time, date, and place, and due to the cause(s) and manner stated.

Signature of certifier: _____

46. NAME, ADDRESS, AND ZIP CODE OF PERSON COMPLETING CAUSE OF DEATH (Item 32)

47. TITLE OF CERTIFIER	48. LICENSE NUMBER	49. DATE CERTIFIED (Mo/Day/Yr)	50. **FOR REGISTRAR ONLY**- DATE FILED (Mo/Day/Yr)

51. DECEDENT'S EDUCATION-Check the box that best describes the highest degree or level of school completed at the time of death. ☐ 8th grade or less ☐ 9th - 12th grade; no diploma ☐ High school graduate or GED completed ☐ Some college credit, but no degree ☐ Associate degree (e.g., AA, AS) ☐ Bachelor's degree (e.g., BA, AB, BS) ☐ Master's degree (e.g., MA, MS, MEng, MEd, MSW, MBA) ☐ Doctorate (e.g., PhD, EdD) or Professional degree (e.g., MD, DDS, DVM, LLB, JD)	52. DECEDENT OF HISPANIC ORIGIN? Check the box that best describes whether the decedent is Spanish/Hispanic/Latino. Check the "No" box if decedent is not Spanish/Hispanic/Latino. ☐ No, not Spanish/Hispanic/Latino ☐ Yes, Mexican, Mexican American, Chicano ☐ Yes, Puerto Rican ☐ Yes, Cuban ☐ Yes, other Spanish/Hispanic/Latino (Specify) _____	53. DECEDENT'S RACE (Check one or more races to indicate what the decedent considered himself or herself to be) ☐ White ☐ Black or African American ☐ American Indian or Alaska Native (Name of the enrolled or principal tribe) _____ ☐ Asian Indian ☐ Chinese ☐ Filipino ☐ Japanese ☐ Korean ☐ Vietnamese ☐ Other Asian (Specify)_____ ☐ Native Hawaiian ☐ Guamanian or Chamorro ☐ Samoan ☐ Other Pacific Islander (Specify)_____ ☐ Other (Specify)_____

54. DECEDENT'S USUAL OCCUPATION (Indicate type of work done during most of working life. DO NOT USE RETIRED).

55. KIND OF BUSINESS/INDUSTRY

Left margin labels: NAME OF DECEDENT—For use by physician or institution; To Be Completed/Verified By: FUNERAL DIRECTOR; To Be Completed By: MEDICAL CERTIFIER; To Be Completed By: FUNERAL DIRECTOR

FIGURE 28.1 The U.S. Standard Certificate of Death. Each state's death certificate is similar, but few are identical to the standard.

Example 1. Natural Death

Part I	Immediate cause: A. **Acute myocardial infarct**	Approximate interval between onset and death **2 days**
	Due to, or as a consequence of: B. **Coronary artery thrombosis**	**2 days**
	Due to, or as a consequence of: C. **Atherosclerotic coronary artery disease**	**Decades**
	Due to, or as a consequence of: D.	
Part II	OTHER SIGNIFICANT CONDITIONS: Conditions contributing to death but not resulting in the underlying cause of death in Part I **Essential Hypertension**	

Example 2. Accidental Death

Part I	A. **Splenic rupture with intra-abdominal hemorrhage**	Approximate interval between onset and death **Minutes**
	Due to, or as a consequence of: B. **Contusion of spleen**	**7 days**
	Due to, or as a consequence of: C. **Blunt force trauma of abdomen**	**7 days**
	Due to, or as a consequence of: D. **Motor vehicle crash**	**7 days**
Part II	OTHER SIGNIFICANT CONDITIONS: Conditions contributing to death but not resulting in the underlying cause of death in Part I	

37. MANNER OF DEATH
    Accident
	38. DATE OF INJURY
	    Jan. 19, 1995
		39. TIME OF INJURY
		    Approx. 2:30 a.m.

40. PLACE OF INJURY
    City street
		41. INJURY AT WORK?
		    No

42. LOCATION OF INJURY
    619 Slippery Trail, Catapolis, Georgia 33996
		43. DESCRIBE HOW INJURY OCCURRED
		    Driving car. Struck curb. Vehicle struck a tree.

FIGURE 28.2 Sample cause-of-death statements that could appear on a death certificate.

29 Exhumations

Exhumation is the act of removing a body from its place of entombment, regardless of whether it is buried or in some sort of a mausoleum. Another word for the process is *disinterment*.

Sometimes it is necessary for the medical examiner or coroner to perform an exhumation. This occurs because an autopsy was not performed prior to burial when one should have been performed, or because additional information comes to light to show that an autopsy performed prior to burial may have been done incorrectly or was inadequate. In many areas the medical examiner or coroner can order an exhumation without a court order, but in some areas the medical examiner or coroner must obtain a court order from a judge to do so.

Interested next of kin may also request that an exhumation and autopsy be performed. For example, a relative may die and be buried without autopsy, then additional information may come up that raises family concerns. The concerns, however, may not cause the medical examiner or coroner to feel it necessary to become involved in the investigation. In such instances, most states have provisions for interested parties to obtain a permit for disinterment. In some areas this may require a court order from a superior court judge, but in many areas a disinterment permit may be obtained from the local or state vital records registrar, who is responsible for filing birth and death certificates. The services of an attorney or funeral director may be required to obtain the permit, but usually obtaining such a permit is not difficult.

It makes sense to require a permit to disinter a body. From the state's standpoint, it is valuable to know when and where bodies are buried and when these burial sites are altered. Imagine what would happen if one could just go out and dig up a body at any time. There needs to be a record to show when grave sites are disturbed and where human remains are ultimately placed.

Exhumations are expensive. If conducted by the coroner or medical examiner, the local government usually foots the bill. However, if a private citizen arranges for an exhumation, there will probably be a fee for opening and closing the grave. There may also be a fee for transport of the body and a requirement on the part of the cemetery for the private citizen to purchase a new vault when the body is reburied. All of this may cost several thousand dollars, let alone the cost of performing an autopsy examination, which involves another professional fee that may vary from hundreds to thousands of dollars.

The arrangements for conducting an autopsy or examination of disinterred remains are essentially the same as those described in the chapter on private death investigations.

Whether an exhumation will be helpful depends on the questions that arise. Under the best of circumstances, even if an autopsy is performed prior to embalming and burial an autopsy cannot answer all questions that arise. Even when bodies are embalmed and buried, they eventually decompose and skeletonize. How fast this occurs depends on the quality of the embalming job, the nature of the soil, and the quality of the casket and nature of the vault in which the body is buried. Before performing an exhumation, it is essential to identify the questions that need to be answered, and then have experts in exhumation determine whether the questions can be answered. You could probably find someone to perform an exhumation, only to find that you had spent a lot of money and still did not have your questions answered. It is highly desirable to identify the questions in advance, and then determine whether it is feasible to perform an exhumation.

Quite often, when an exhumation is performed, the funeral home that handled the original funeral arrangements and burial will make arrangements to disinter the body and reinter it at a later date. The funeral home will also probably be involved in the transport of the body, opening of the casket, and replacement of the remains in the casket.

It is important when an exhumation is performed to engage the services of a pathologist who has experience at exhumations. Many artifacts occur during the decomposition of the body that require special expertise to interpret. Hospital pathologists who are used to examining bodies in the freshly dead state, may not be capable of adequately assessing the findings in an exhumed body. Because questions often arise regarding the presence or absence of injuries, it is highly desirable to utilize a forensic pathologist experienced in examining exhumed remains.

30 Death Investigation and Funeral Arrangements

Funeral directors usually like to obtain a dead body as soon as possible after death. The longer a body sits after death, even if it is refrigerated, the more the appearance of the body changes and the more difficult it is to make the body appear natural. Persons who conduct death investigations are aware of such needs and, in general, do the best they can to have the body available to the funeral home in a timely manner. However, no matter what type of death investigation is conducted, the procedure may delay delivery of the body to the funeral home. Usually this does not involve delays of more than a day. Most places that conduct death investigations have the capability of embalming the body prior to an autopsy if necessary, although embalming can induce artifacts that make autopsy findings difficult to interpret. In most instances, however, embalming a body prior to autopsy is neither needed nor desired, and the body can be returned to the funeral home in a timely fashion. Most states have regulations that require the body to be returned to the custody of the family or to the funeral home within a specified time following death or autopsy — usually one to several days. In cases in which the body may need to be maintained for a longer period of time, regulations usually also permit an extension if the medical examiner or coroner requests one. In most instances, however, examination of the body will be conducted the same day or the day following death, or after permission for examination is obtained, depending on the type of death investigation, and the body will be released in a timely fashion.

Regardless of the type of death investigation, the usual autopsy will not involve incisions into areas of the body that will be visible if the body is to be displayed for funeral services. Standard incisions are made in the scalp, in the chest, and the abdomen, and these can be easily closed, concealed, sealed, and processed with cosmetics to make them inconspicuous or invisible. Although many people attribute the different appearance of a body at the funeral home to autopsy-related procedures, most of these changes are more related to the embalming process itself and the natural processes the body goes through after death. Let's face it, the characteristics that make a person appear alive, such as the gleam in their eyes, the smile on their face, and the position of their eyebrows, changes after death. Even the best of funeral directors cannot recreate human personality and characteristics.

In most medicolegal death investigations, when an autopsy is performed, the only specimens that are kept are those that are needed for diagnostic or evidence purposes. In general, most of the organs are returned to the body for transport to the funeral home with the body. Because many institution-based autopsies are performed in teaching institutions, when autopsies are conducted in hospitals outside of the medicolegal death investigation system, it is not uncommon for the organs to be retained by the hospital so they may be used for research or teaching purposes. In general, the autopsy permit forms in such situations will explain that the organs will be retained and that they may be used for teaching and other purposes. In medicolegal death investigations, if specimens are retained for teaching or research purposes, special permission may be required from the next of kin. Most state laws only enable the medical examiner and coroner to keep those specimens that are required for diagnosis or evidence.

The custom of medicolegal death investigators returning the organs to the body is probably an outgrowth of the fact that there may be a need for a second opinion or examination of the organs or body by another party or at another time. Returning the organs to the body allows them to be preserved so that if other medicolegal issues come up at a later time, there is something left to examine. Sometimes, however, organs or specimens must be retained for further diagnosis or as evidence, and they may not be sent to the funeral home with the body. In institution-based death investigations and autopsies, those organs not kept for teaching and research purposes are usually incinerated at the hospital or by a company that specializes in the disposal of biological waste. Whether organs are retained in a private death investigation will depend on the needs of the case.

There is a common misconception that embalming is required by law. In most states, embalming is not required by law unless the body is to be transported across state lines or by air. Some states require embalming when certain infectious disease conditions are present. Requirements for embalming are usually not a matter of state law, but may be required by cemeteries in order to be buried. Many cemeteries require that bodies buried on the premises be either cremated or embalmed. Some people may wish to save money and reduce funeral expenses by not having a dead body embalmed, but the bulk of funeral expenses are related to services, the casket, the vault, and opening and closing of the grave; embalming is a relatively small portion of the total cost. If cost considerations are important for burial, cremation is probably the least expensive route to make final disposition of a body. Most states do not require the burial of cremated remains, thus creating the potential for eliminating substantial expense. Most states will allow the dispersion of what are called *cremains* into lakes, woods, or other areas, as long as it is specified on the death certificate where the ashes or cremains are to be distributed. For additional details concerning funeral and burial, you may wish to contact a local funeral director.

31 Principles of Evidence

During a death investigation, one never really knows what might constitute important evidence. It might be something as simple as a loose hair on a piece of clothing or a phone number written on a piece of paper in the decedent's pocket. When legal proceedings occur, regardless of whether they are criminal or civil trials or proceedings, evidence is used by attorneys to support their side of the case. It is important that medical examiners, coroners, and other death investigators be aware of potentially important evidence and that they know what to do with it when it is encountered.

First of all, evidence must be *recognized*. Persons performing a death investigation must be aware that something they see or find might constitute potential evidence. Much of the education and training in death investigation teaches people how to recognize things that might constitute potential evidence.

Once a piece of evidence is recognized, a decision must be made as to whether to *obtain* it — that is, should it be collected? In most instances, any piece of potential evidence is collected (obtained) in case it is needed at a later time during the investigation.

Once an item of evidence is obtained, then it must be *preserved* in an appropriate way. Preservation may involve something as simple as placing it in a sealed container, although specific types of evidence often require specific preservation techniques. For example, some types of blood specimens are best preserved by drying them and keeping them dry until subsequent tests can be performed, while other tests may have to be done on wet blood. Placing certain items of evidence in fluid, for example, might cause them to dissolve. Preservation of evidence is a critical issue and persons in death investigation are, in general, trained in methods of properly preserving evidence once it has been recognized and obtained.

The next stage in evidence processing is that of *transmission*. Remember the rake analogy where one person often collects evidence and gives it to another person. Evidence must be properly transmitted to ensure its integrity. For example, a substance that is sensitive to heat might be transmitted in a refrigerated package to keep it from becoming altered. Again, death investigators must be familiar with the proper ways of transmitting evidence so it is not destroyed or altered in the process.

The last stage related to evidence has to do with *analyzing* it. Once the proper person receives the evidence, analysis consists of examination and testing of the evidence to document its qualities and to better describe its nature.

Thus, the stages of evidence processing include *recognition, obtainment, preservation, transmission*, and *analysis* (Figure 31.1).

An important concept related to evidence is called the *chain of custody*. In order to be used in most legal proceedings, there must be documentation that the evidence has not been altered by anyone, and it must be able to be shown who had the evidence at any particular point in time. Thus, during the various stages of evidence processing,

Steps Involved in Evidence Processing

Recognition	The pathologist must recognize that a particular object or substance may be important evidence and needs to be collected or documented, such as being photographed.
Obtaining	The evidence then needs to be collected (or photographed) so that it may be reviewed or analyzed by others.
Preserving	The evidence must be stored and packaged in such a way that its is not destroyed or contaminated.
Transmission	The evidence must be transported or transferred in such a way that its integrity is preserved and the chain of custody is documented.
Analysis	The evidence is analyzed by a forensic scientist trained and qualified to analyze the type of evidence provided.

FIGURE 31.1 There are various steps in the processing of evidence that are common to all cases, as shown here. Sometimes evidence may consist of a photograph (or digital image) of a distinctive finding, such as a patterned injury or blood spatter pattern, which cannot actually be collected in a practical way. In such cases, the photograph becomes the evidence that must be protected in the same way as any other evidence.

there must be a documentation of the chain of custody. This usually involves having each person who handles the evidence designate what the evidence is, sign for it, and have the date, time, and person to whom it is transported also sign for it when it is received. Thus, there is a paper trail or other documentary record that shows where the evidence was at any particular time, who had it, and any dates and times when it was transferred from one person or agency to another. Failure to adequately document the chain of custody can result in evidence not being allowed to be admitted in court or other legal proceedings. Some courts are rather lenient with chain of custody regulations and others are very strict. In general, it is necessary to document the chain of custody and let the legal system figure out whether or not the evidence is admissible or not.

Another type of concept related to evidence is that of *class* and *unique charac-teristics*. Much of the useful aspect of evidence has to do with pattern recognition or being able to match a suspected piece of evidence to a known source. For example, does this blood come from a specific person? Was this bullet fired from this gun? Does this tire tread mark match the tire on this vehicle? The list of such questions goes on, but the basic principle is the same. Most efforts are expended at trying to identify the nature of a piece of evidence and where or who it came from.

A *class characteristic* is a characteristic of a specific piece of evidence that places it into a general category. For example, there may be a tire tread imprint on a person who has been run over by a car. Recognizing the imprint as a tire tread mark places it into the general class of tire tread marks, but there are many tires that have the same kind of treads. So simply placing it into a tire tread mark class does not enable identification of the specific tire that made the tread mark. Class characteristics can fall at different levels. For example, a general class characteristic might be that the marking is a tire tread mark. A more specific class characteristic might be that the tread mark matches only those tires that are made by Michelin. Still, there are many Michelin tires on the road, and the need may arise to identify a specific tire that made the mark.

As you might imagine, tires might be somewhat like fingerprints. Although they might be all very similar when they were first put on automobiles, their pattern of wear, the running over of objects, and other defects on the tire may create marks that are unique to a specific, single, individual tire that is different from all other tires. Such characteristics constitute a *unique characteristic*, which enables the evidence to be matched to a specific source. There are many types of evidence that lend themselves to the identification of unique characteristics. The distinctive markings left by a specific gun on a bullet is one. A patterned bruise made by a specific chain might be another. You can probably imagine many other examples that could be used to point out the difference between a general class characteristic and a unique characteristic of a given piece of evidence.

The types of evidence that are commonly analyzed include blood (for typing or toxicology testing), bullets, tissue samples (evaluated for microscopic and other findings indicative of disease or injury), clothing, hairs, fibers, and foreign materials such as metal fragments or glass shards that are found in wounds. This is just a sampling of things that are often regarded as evidence.

Evidence is usually documented in several ways. Quite commonly it is photographed. Items that are obtained as evidence are usually described in the various death investigation reports. In addition, each item of evidence is usually labeled as to what it is or where it came from, along with a unique identification number belonging to the specific death investigation case. Adequate documentation of the evidence is necessary to appropriately preserve the chain of custody.

Evidence may be kept for many years. Most state crime laboratories, medical examiner's offices, and coroner's offices have policies and procedures they follow regarding how long evidence is kept. Eventually, however, usually due to storage problems or resolution of a case through trial or other legal proceedings, evidence may ultimately be destroyed or discarded.

32 What Is an Expert?

The definition of an expert is not uniform in its application. For example, there may be a physician who is recognized by his or her peers as being an expert in a specialty area and who has more knowledge about a particular topic than any other physician. This type of expert is *professionally recognized*. However in the court system, the definition of an expert is somewhat different.

In the court setting, an expert is a person who has, through education or experience, more knowledge about a particular subject than the *average person*. In the court setting, a person is not defined as an expert by his peers or people who do the same type of work, but rather by the court system and the judge. The attorneys present the qualifications and experience of a witness being put forth as a possible expert, and the court considers these qualifications and then makes a decision whether or not to allow the person to testify as an expert. Expert witnesses are different than the normal witness or so-called *fact witness*. A *fact witness* is only allowed to testify to things they saw, did, or know, such as their observations. They are not permitted to testify as to their opinion regarding what may have happened or what they think about certain issues. In contrast, an expert is allowed to use his or her professional knowledge to render opinions about certain facts that go beyond simple testimony about what he or she saw, did, or observed (Figure 32.1).

The expert witness may sound like a straightforward concept, but the way in which people are determined to be experts by the court may result in circumstances where they are permitted to testify about subjects for which they are not truly experts. For example, a toxicologist may be qualified as an expert to testify about blood alcohol levels, and in doing so may be allowed to testify about alcohol's effects on the brain and the human body, when in fact he or she has limited knowledge of that area, and is more familiar with how the test is performed from a technical standpoint. As another example, in some courts a pathologist may be qualified as an expert and be allowed to testify about the quality of surgery that was done on a particular person, when in fact the pathologist does not have any real experience in surgical practice. As you might imagine, such occurrences may cast into doubt the validity of an expert witness's testimony or opinions. There have been efforts in some states to require that experts be actively engaged in the field in which they are going to testify and that they meet certain criteria. However, attorneys, and many physicians, have opposed such legislation for various reasons, and in most places the expert witness is qualified as described above, based on knowledge that is simply more than that of the average person.

In one case, several different dentists testified about an alleged bite mark on a dead body. One dentist testified that it was not a bite mark; one testified that it was, but it was not human. Another dentist testified that it was human but that it could

Types of Witnesses

Fact Witness	A fact witness is permitted to testify only to facts such as things the witness did or observed. The fact witness may not offer opinions.
Expert Witness	If qualified by the court as an expert witness, the witness may use his/her expertise to offer opinions. Forensic pathologists often serve as expert witnesses.

FIGURE 32.1 Although medical examiners, coroners, and forensic pathologists may be called to testify only as fact witnesses (answering simple questions such as "Did you perform an autopsy?" or "Did you remove a bullet?") it is more common for them to testify as expert witnesses, in which case the witness may offer opinions about things such as how long it may have taken a person to die after being injured.

not be matched to a specific person. The court ended up throwing out all of the testimony, but there was considerable expense and controversy created by the testimony in the first place. One could argue that it might be better to screen such experts and evaluate their proposed testimony in advance, and when appropriate, not allow the testimony in the first place.

There are numerous other examples of expert testimony causing problems in court and legal proceedings, but it is beyond the scope of this book to discuss them fully. The major thrust of this chapter is to point out that the so-called expert in forensic science may, in fact, have limited expertise. Professional organizations are gradually dealing with these issues as the ethics committees within these organizations often get complaints filed about expert witness testimony and the credentials of experts, which are sometimes falsified or overstated.

The medical examiner or coroner may be involved in such dilemmas about whether or not they really have expertise in a given area. Because of the broad-based nature and scope of knowledge they need to conduct death investigations, medical examiners and coroners are often asked questions that involve issues they know a little bit about, but may not have complete expertise in the topic. As an example, forensic pathologists are often asked about different types of bullets and issues related to guns. A forensic pathologist may be familiar with some of these issues and can be capable of competently answering some questions, but in other areas may not be qualified to answer the questions. Some people, either intentionally or unintentionally, get drawn into answering questions they should not or cannot knowledgeably answer. The bottom line is that expert testimony and opinions should be viewed with caution and circumspection, and one should always question whether a so-called expert is really an expert.

33 What If You Disagree?

At some point in your life, if it has not happened already, you will probably become personally involved in a death investigation. That is, you may have a vested interest in the outcome of the death investigation. For example, assume that you are at a friend's house and are preparing to go hunting. Your friend tells you that he is going downstairs to clean his gun. A few minutes later you hear a shot and rush downstairs and find him dead on the floor. The coroner comes to the scene, conducts a death investigation, and the death certificate indicates that the manner of death is suicide. You disagree and believe that his death was accidental. What do you do?

The first step, when one disagrees with the outcome of a death investigation, is to go to the source of the information. Usually that is the person who is officially responsible for conducting the death investigation. This procedure holds true regardless of whether the death investigation is medicolegal, institution-based, or private. Controversies and questions can usually be resolved by a one-on-one discussion with the person who is officially in charge of the death investigation.

If, after discussing concerns with the source, there is still dissatisfaction, it may be valuable to obtain a second opinion. Most medical examiners and coroners are familiar with individuals who can offer second opinions on death investigations, and it may be worthwhile to place a call to the medical examiner or coroner, even one that did not conduct the initial investigation, in order to get referrals to people who might be able to help you. Another method is to call a local hospital and ask for a pathologist who might be able to refer you to an appropriate person. An attorney might also be able to help, but there may be fees involved. Of course, no matter who you get to offer a second opinion, there will probably be some sort of a professional fee involved for the time spent in reviewing the case and offering an opinion. This may vary from a few hundred dollars to several thousand dollars, depending on the case.

In lieu of immediately obtaining a second opinion, if discussions with the source of the original death investigation information cannot resolve the questions you have, many states have what is referred to as an *administrative remedy*. This is a system within the government to address public complaints that go through a formalized review. Administrative remedy occurs outside the court system and does not require a lawsuit. In essence, a complaint is raised, it is referred to appropriate agencies within the government, appropriate witnesses render statements and opinions, and some board or agency reviews the materials and makes an ultimate decision in the case. Using the administrative remedy system may save money and avoid the need to go to court.

Rarely, medical examiners or coroners have been sued. Typical examples of such lawsuits have resulted when a medical examiner or coroner certifies a death as being due to suicide, but family members believe strongly that death is due to accidental or perhaps even homicidal causes. In most instances, however, court decisions have favored the medical examiner's or coroner's viewpoint, especially if there is no evidence that the medical examiner was incompetent, arbitrary, or capricious, and there is evidence that the medical examiner operated according to standard procedures and in good faith. In a number of states it may not even be possible to successfully sue the medical examiner or coroner because they, acting as agents of the government, may be considered immune from civil liability because their duties are discretionary and quasi-judicial in nature. If communication with the medical examiner or coroner is initiated, issues can usually be resolved without the need for legal action.

It needs to be emphasized that most concerns can be addressed by a one-on-one conversation with the person who is officially responsible for conducting the death investigation. If you have complaints or questions, call the person who conducted the investigation, set up an appointment, and go talk to him or her. Most medical examiners and coroners are good people who are honest and objective and will tell you the limitations and reasons behind what they do. Most are compassionate and understanding and will try to help address concerns that arise.

The same general procedures can be followed regardless of whether you disagree with the outcome of a medicolegal death investigation, an institution-based investigation, or a private death investigation, except that administrative remedy, if available, may apply only to official (medicolegal) death investigations.

34 Death Investigation and Insurance Policies

Life insurance companies use death investigation information when they process life insurance claims, but they do not usually take the death investigation or autopsy report information at face value. In fact, most major insurance companies now conduct their own investigations (although much of it is simply the reviewing of available information) and formulate their own opinions as to the cause, manner, and circumstances of death.

Historically there have been several issues that routinely interest insurance companies regarding deaths. One is the accidental death clause or the *double indemnity clause*. Many insurance policies will pay double the face value of the policy amount if death was due to accidental causes. This often results in disputes about whether a death was truly accidental. The definition of *accident* may be quite different to the insurance company than it is to the medical examiner or coroner. Just because the death certificate says that the death was accidental does not necessarily mean that the insurance company will pay accidental death benefits. For example, a person may die of an accidental drug overdose after illegally using cocaine. The insurance company may not pay accidental death benefits because illegal drug abuse was involved in causing the death.

Another common issue relates to suicide. Many insurance policies have a *suicide exclusion cause* that negates the policy or reduces the benefit if suicide occurs within a specified time of the policy being instituted — two years is a common figure. Quite often, the medical examiner or coroner may have suspicions that a death is suicidal, but there is inadequate evidence to meet the criteria for calling the death a suicide. Thus, the medical examiner or coroner may certify the death as an accident, but the insurance company may develop evidence that convinces the medical examiner or cornoner that the death was suicidal.

When more than one person dies at a time, particularly if it is a husband and wife, the inheritance of their estate may be dependent on who died first. The information developed in the death investigation may be heavily relied upon to determine which beneficiaries get what part of the estate. Some states have legislation that specifically details what happens when a husband and wife die in the same incident and it cannot be determined who died first. As you might imagine, such a law may indicate the estate is processed under the assumption that the people died at the same time, and essentially the estates are split.

Another aspect of death investigation involves opinions about how long the conditions that led to death existed prior to death. Although not all medical examiners, coroners, and physicians complete this item on the death certificate, insurance companies may need this information. Many insurance policies have provisions that relate to preexisting conditions (illnesses), and if it can be shown that a condition existed prior to the purchase of the insurance policy and death results from that condition, the insurance policy may not pay at all or may pay a reduced death benefit. Thus, the information stated on the death certificate (or in other records assembled by medical examiners and coroners) may play an important role in this evaluation process.

Another aspect of insurance relates to the detection of drugs in decedents. Many insurance policies will negate payment of the death benefit or reduce it if death is brought about or hastened by drug abuse. Of course, as previously mentioned, it is a routine part of a death investigation, particularly a medicolegal death investigation, to evaluate for the presence of drugs of abuse and other commonly abused drugs.

Finally, another aspect of the insurance business that impacts death investigation relates to the fact that insurance payoffs are sometimes a motive for murder. When deaths occur under suspicious circumstances, medicolegal death investigators sometimes inquire about the nature of insurance policies as they may shed some light on the circumstances surrounding the death. For example, the death of a person who has apparently committed suicide becomes suspicious if a large insurance policy was taken out on the deceased just a few months before death.

An important point to remember is that whatever the outcome of the death investigation, insurance companies may disagree. Even if the results of a death investigation somehow benefit you, the insurance payments may not, and vice versa.

35 Classic Dilemmas in Death Investigation

Although you might imagine that medical examiners and coroners all follow the same procedures and do things essentially the same way, such a world has not been attained. Medical examiners, coroners, and death investigators are people, and they have individual preferences and approaches to problems. This means that two deaths in two different areas of the country that occur under virtually identical circumstances may not be investigated or certified in exactly the same way. What follows is a description of some of the more typical cases of this type.

When a person dies from playing Russian roulette, in which a partially loaded revolver is placed to the head and the trigger is pulled, not knowing whether the gun will discharge, most medicolegal death investigation offices certify such deaths as suicides. However, some offices regard them as accidents.

Deaths resulting from complications of medical procedures pose another problem. For example, if a person was undergoing catheterization and the catheter perforates an artery and causes a fatal hemorrhage, some medical examiners and coroners regard these as accidental deaths while others regard them as natural deaths.

Drug-related deaths are also handled inconsistently. Many medical examiners and coroners regard a drug overdose as an accidental death (as long as there was no evidence of suicide), while others classify such a death as undetermined in manner because the decedent's intent may be unclear.

Combinations of natural disease and injury or external causes also pose problems. For example, when a man has a heart attack while swimming and then drowns, some people regard these as accidental deaths, while others regard them as natural.

Forced police shootings pose yet another problem. Imagine a man who has threatened suicide and has barricaded himself in his home, causing a great disturbance and the neighbors call the police. The police come to the house and try to calm the man down but are unsuccessful. Ultimately a confrontation takes place in which the man tells the police that if they don't go away, he will shoot himself. He then, however, charges toward the police as if he is going to shoot them and they are forced to shoot him. In the process, he dies. Some medical examiners and coroners would regard this as a suicide while others would regard it as a homicide.

Cocaine-related deaths are yet another example of inconsistent practices. Sometimes when a person abuses cocaine, he or she will develop a small blockage in one of his coronary arteries and suffer a fatal cardiac rhythm disturbance. This is not truly an overdose case where an excessive amount of the drug was ingested. It is an idiosyncratic reaction to the drug cocaine. Some medical examiners and coroners would regard this as accidental, while others would regard it as natural.

A Guide
For
Manner of Death
Classification

First Edition

National Association of Medical Examiners ®

Prepared by
Randy Hanzlick, MD
John C. Hunsaker III, MD, JD
Gregory J. Davis, MD

Approved by the NAME Board of Directors
February 2002

FIGURE 35.1 In 2002, the National Association of Medical Examiners published its *Guide for Manner of Death Classification*. The *Guide* was developed in recognition that the classification of manner of death varied somewhat from place to place, and a goal of the guide is to foster more consistency in manner of death classification. The *Guide* discusses, in detail, many issues related to manner of death, and includes many of the commonly encountered death scenarios that pose dilemmas for medical examiners and coroners who must classify the manner of death as homicide, suicide, accident, natural, or undetermined. The *Guide* is available for viewing at www.TheNAME.org.

Food allergies pose a problem. Assume that a man knows that he is allergic to shellfish. He goes out to a restaurant and orders a dinner in which he is unaware that shellfish are present in the mixture of food. While eating dinner, he has a severe allergic reaction and dies. Many people would regard this as a natural death, while others would regard it as accidental.

Another example involves deaths in which fear causes death. Imagine that a teenager goes up to an elderly gentleman's house on Halloween, sees him sitting in the living room, jumps up in the window, and yells "Boo." Immediately thereafter the man stands up, collapses, and dies. Again, some people would call this an accidental death, some would call it homicide, and a few might even call it natural.

Deaths following trivial injury are also difficult. Imagine a man who gets in an argument with his girlfriend, who bites him. He gets mad, runs over to his brother's house, and while explaining what happened, collapses and dies. Again, opinion varies as to whether this is natural, accidental, or homicidal in nature.

These are but a few examples of potential inconsistencies in death investigation outcome and certification practice. As you can see, most of the time the discrepancies relate to the manner of death rather than the cause of death. In each of the instances above, the cause of death is fairly apparent. It is the manner of death that is controversial. Just imagine the effect that varying practices have on the statistics in the United States when deaths such as those above are classified differently in different locations. To foster more consistency in approach, the National Association of Medical Examiners has developed guidelines for manner of death classification, which are available on the web at www.TheNAME.org. (See Figure 35.1 on opposite page.)

The major take-home point is that you should not assume that all medical examiners and coroners follow the same procedures. In some cases their approaches vary not only with respect to death investigation, but also in how deaths are ultimately certified in terms of cause and manner. A major reason for this is that the medical examiner or coroner must have some discretion to use his or her professional judgment.

36 Professional Death Investigation Organizations

There are only a few national organizations that are directly involved with death investigation issues in the U.S. A general description of each one is provided below.

The National Association of Medical Examiners (NAME) is based in Atlanta, GA, and was established in 1966. Originally located in New York City, the headquarters moved to Wilmington, DE, then to St. Louis, and then to Atlanta in 2003. The membership of this organization consists primarily of medical examiners who are physicians, although physician coroners also qualify for membership. There is an affiliate category of membership for the office administrators and investigators who work in medical examiners' and coroners' offices. NAME has an annual meeting at which they conduct their business and present scientific presentations and this meeting usually occurs in September or October of each year. In addition, it usually has a one-day interim meeting in February, during the week in which the American Academy of Forensic Sciences meeting is held (see below). The total membership of the National Association of Medical Examiners is approximately 800 individuals of which about 150 are affiliates and the rest are full medical examiner members. The organization addresses issues that are relevant to medical examiner practices, including the development of standards and guidelines, and they also respond to general issues that affect medical examiners and coroners. The association is the official sponsor of the *American Journal of Forensic Medicine and Pathology*, which has numerous articles concerning death investigation issues and is published four times per year. An internet discussion group called NAME-L is also used by the membership, and NAME has a web site at www.TheNAME.org.

The American Academy of Forensic Sciences (AAFS) was established in 1948 and is now based in Colorado Springs, CO. This organization has more than 5000 members representing all of the disciplines in the forensic sciences. The academy is set up in sections that conduct their own business meetings and scientific sessions. These sections include pathology-biology, toxicology, criminalistics, questioned documents, jurisprudence, engineering, and psychiatry/behavioral science, anthropology, odontology, and general. The specific roles of the people in these sections are further defined in Chapter 14. AAFS has an annual meeting each February at various locations around the country. It is the sponsoring organization of the *Journal of Forensic Sciences*, which contains various articles related to death investigation and forensic science. The AAFS puts out a bimonthly newsletter called the *Academy*

News, which is available to members and can be obtained for a nominal fee. AAFS also has a web site at www.aafs.org.

The International Association of Coroners and Medical Examiners (IACME) consists primarily of coroners, but some medical examiners are also members. The IACME has an annual meeting. Its membership is not large in comparison to the more than 2000 people who serve as coroners in the United States. The IACME has a website at www.theiacme.com/.

The College of American Pathologists (CAP) is a professional organization of pathologists of all types. It does, however, have a forensic pathology committee and an autopsy committee, which address professional issues related to the autopsy and death investigation. It has produced handbooks and manuals on the topic and also produces guidelines in these areas. The College of American Pathologists is based in Northfield, IL, and is a very large organization that deals with all aspects of the practice of pathology, ranging from the day-to-day diagnostic dilemmas to the business aspect of medical practice management. The autopsy and forensic pathology committees are only a small part of the overall CAP program. The website is www.cap.org.

The American Society of Clinical Pathology (ASCP) is also a professional organization of pathologists, many of whom deal with the laboratory aspects of pathology rather than the autopsy. However, the society also has a forensic pathology program that produces educational materials and continuing medical education materials for forensic pathologists. The ASCP is based in Chicago, Illinois, and includes a very large membership that consists of not only pathologists, but many of the technologists and technicians who work in hospital and other types of laboratories. Again, the death investigation activities of the ASCP are relatively small compared to the overall programs of the organization. The website is www.ascp.org.

The American Board of Medicolegal Death Investigators (ABMDI), based in St. Louis, MO, has developed training curricula and examinations, so that death investigators may become registered or certified. Most diplomates of this organization are non-physician death investigators who work in medical examiner's or coroner's offices. The web site is www.slu.edu/organizations/abmdi/.

The American Board of Pathology (ABP) is a professional board established to credential people in the various areas of pathology. It establishes rules and regulations regarding what types of pathology training are acceptable. It also creates examinations in the many different fields of pathology, which pathologists may take to become board certified pathologists. The ABP is composed of pathologists who examine their peers in order to show that a person has obtained at least a minimum level of competence. The ABP offers a specific test in forensic pathology. After a physician has gone through the required number of years of training in an educational program that meets the board's requirements, the pathologist may sit for the examination. Once qualified to take the examination, the individual is referred to as being *board qualified*. If the examination is successfully completed (i.e. the pathologist passes the examination), then that person is designated as *board certified*. Being board certified indicates that a given pathologist has followed a standard set of training guidelines, spent a specified amount of time in training, and has successfully passed an examination offered by peers. The website is www.abpath.org.

NAME, AAFS, CAP, IACME, and ASCP are membership organizations, meaning that people pay to belong to the organization. ABP and ABMDI are certifying organizations that provide testing so that qualified individuals may become certified in their discipline. There are fees for the examinations, but people do not belong to the organization in the true sense of a membership organization. Many other forensic science organizations exist, but are not as directly involved with death investigation, especially from the medical, pathology, or death investigator standpoints. A few such organizations are the International Association for Identification (IAI), Society of Forensic Toxicologists (SOFT), and The International Association of Forensic Toxicologists (TIAFT).

The American Academy of Forensic Sciences has developed some new programs that touch on the topics of certification and accreditation. The Forensic Education Programs Accreditation Commission (FEPAC) was established to review institutional education programs in forensic science to ensure that they meet certain standards. The Forensic Specialties Accreditation Board was established to review procedures of various bodies who offer certifications to individuals, to make sure that the certification bodies meet certain standards.

37 Access to Death Investigation Information

In a private death investigation, the information generated from the investigation belongs to the family or person who arranged for and authorized the death investigation. Copies should not be provided by anyone without the knowledge and consent of the authorizing person.

The information generated in an institution-based death investigation usually becomes part of the patient's medical record and is subject to the same confidentiality procedures as the medical record. Although the patient's physician or the institution may use the medical record, third parties may not usually obtain the medical record without an authorization from the legal next of kin.

The information generated in a medicolegal death investigation is handled differently among the states. Some states regard such reports as confidential, while others have an *open records* or *sunshine* law that makes such documents public records that are available to anyone who asks for them, or through the freedom of information process. Still other states fall in between, where the person requesting the information must have some legitimate interest in the death.

Freedom of information acts and open records acts, have provided access to official records for parties not directly involved in a specific case, but specific procedures must be followed which may vary by state.

Some life insurance policies require that if an autopsy is performed, the insurance company has a right to obtain a copy of the report for its own use. It is prudent to be familiar with the provisions of your insurance policy.

No matter what type of death investigation is conducted, the information is always potentially subject to disclosure through a legal process such as a court order or subpoena.

38 Pronouncement of Death

A body is often not considered legally dead until death is *pronounced*. Pronouncement is an official declaration by a qualified person that death has occurred, and the date, time, and place of pronouncement are documented on the death certificate and in other places. In most states, a person must be pronounced dead by a physician, although in some areas, medical personnel such as nurses are allowed to pronounce. In other areas, lay coroners are permitted to pronounce death, especially if death is obvious, such as when decapitation occurs or when the body is a skeleton or badly decomposed.

The requirement that a physician pronounce death stems from the fact that it is often difficult to determine if, or to be sure that, a person is dead. This fact accounts for the horror stories we occasionally hear about people "waking up" in body bags or at the morgue, or being left for dead only to survive. Physician involvement also causes some logistic problems because a physician is not always available at the place where death occurs. As a result it is sometimes necessary for a dead body to be transported to a nearby emergency room, where a physician can pronounce death. As you can imagine, such transport takes time and may delay the delivery of a body to the funeral home, medical examiner's office, or other location. Of course if a physician medical examiner or coroner is at the death scene, that person might pronounce death.

As you can see, the *official* date, place, and time of death (i.e., date, time, and place pronounced) might differ from the *actual* date, time, and place pronounced. It is important to understand the difference because insurance policies or other administrative activities related to death may rely on the details of pronouncement rather than the actual or estimated time of death. Imagine what might happen if someone who was going to leave you a bunch of money when he died, actually died at 11:30 PM, but was pronounced at 12:30 AM the next morning, and the life insurance policy expired at midnight! You might be out a lot of money. It sounds far-fetched, but such things occasionally happen.

39 Deaths in Custody and Public Institutions

Most states have laws that require notification of the medical examiner or coroner when deaths of prison inmates or other people in police custody occur. The same applies to patients at state or local government institutions, such as mental health facilities and similar institutions. Medicolegal investigation of such deaths fulfills two important tasks. One, investigation can help determine whether there has been some maltreatment, abuse, or injury to such patients in order to protect the public (patients). Two, the information gained can be used to address allegations (founded or unfounded) that abuse, maltreatment, or injury occurred, serving to protect the institution and its staff as well.

Most states do not require notification of the medical examiner or coroner when a death occurs in home-care facilities, hospices, and other such private agencies that render care to terminally ill patients unless some other aspect of the death would require it to be reported. The same holds true for nursing homes. Most states do not have laws that require reporting of nursing home deaths to the medical examiner or coroner, although there is a trend in that direction.

40 Criminal and Civil Law Issues

Most medicolegal death investigation laws are geared toward the investigation of deaths that may involve a crime, such as murder. When such cases come to trial, the proceedings are known as *criminal law* proceedings. In most areas, about 90% of such cases never come to trial, usually because the accused person pleads guilty (common) or because no suspect has been found (uncommon). The remaining 10% or so of cases ultimately progress to a criminal trial. As slow as the legal system is, it is a good thing that not all cases come to trial because there simply would not be time to have all those trials.

Many deaths result in legal proceedings but do not involve a crime. When someone may be responsible (culpable), in whole or in part, for the death of another person through some act of commission (something that was done) or omission (something that was *not* done), there is often a *civil law* proceeding (lawsuit) filed

Criminal Law and Civil Law

Criminal Law	•Involves a violation of law such as murder, robbery, theft, assault, battery, rape •Charges are brought against the defendant by a District Attorney or similar prosecuting attorney •The burden of proof is "beyond a reasonable doubt" •The jury verdict must be unanimous among all jurors
Civil Law	•Involves an alleged "damage" or "tort" that does not involve a violation of the law •A "Plaintiff" files suit to sue another party •The burden of proof is the "preponderance of evidence" •The jury verdict does not require agreement of all jurors

FIGURE 40.1 Most often, because they perform autopsies on homicide victims, medical examiners and coroners testify in cases involving criminal law, in criminal court. However, some deaths result in civil lawsuits in which one party seeks compensation from another for damages that result from some culpability or negligence, but not necessarily from a violation of law. Such cases are often heard in civil court, and it is not uncommon for a medical examiner or coroner to be called to testify as a witness in such cases.

by one person to recover money or other restitution for damages. For example, someone might sue a bank because a family member slipped on a wet floor, hit his or her head, fractured the skull, and died. No crime was committed, but the bank might be held liable (culpable) for not providing a safe environment for customers. Medical examiners and coroners often get involved in such cases because many cases, like this one, involve an injury, which usually qualifies the death for medicolegal death investigation by the medical examiner or coroner.

Thus, medical examiners and coroners are often involved with issues of *criminal law* and *civil law*. (Refer to Figure 40.1 on the previous page.) Their testimony, findings, and opinions are often crucial to the outcome of such legal proceedings.

41 Sample Autopsy Report

This chapter covers the type of information that is usually included in an autopsy report. The format used for autopsy reports varies among hospitals and among the offices of coroners and medical examiners.

REASON FOR PERFORMING AN EXAMINATION

This 57-year-old black male complained of severe headache shortly after intercourse. He was driven to Anywhere County Hospital by his wife, and he became unresponsive shortly after arrival in the emergency room. During resuscitation, difficulty was encountered when attempting to place a subclavian central pressure line, requiring multiple attempts. Total hospital course was confined to the emergency room and the duration was 47 minutes. At the clinician's request, an autopsy is performed to determine the cause of death and establish whether iatrogenic chest or vascular injury is present.

DATE AND TIME OF EXAMINATION

With the consent of the decedent's wife, who was determined by Social Services to be the legal next of kin, an autopsy is performed in the Anywhere County Hospital morgue on Tuesday, November 5, 1991, 16 hours postmortem, and commencing at 12:05 PM with the assistance of Audrey Smith. In attendance for a portion of the examination was Major Gleet, M.D., the medical resident who managed the patient in the emergency room. Permission for complete autopsy with no restrictions was granted.

POSTMORTEM X-RAYS

No postmortem radiographic studies were performed.

PRESENTATION, CLOTHING, AND PERSONAL EFFECTS

The body is wrapped in a white plastic hospital shroud and the hands have been tied at the wrists with string such that the hands rest on the abdomen. A pair of white briefs are present in the pelvic area and these are partially stained with soaked-in blood and have been partially cut away from the body. A gold colored band is present on the left ring finger. The briefs are discarded and the ring is left in place and forwarded with the body.

FEATURES OF IDENTIFICATION

A hospital band on the right wrist and a paper tag attached to the right thumb each bear the name Rigley Mortis. The body is unembalmed and that of a black male appearing slightly older than the stated age. Height measures 68 inches, and estimated weight is 160 pounds. The physique is mesomorphic.

The head hair is black, coarse, measures about one inch in greatest length, and shows fronto-parietal balding. The irides are brown. The teeth are natural with some amalgam restorations. An oblique, well-healed, 4 inch scar with cross-hatched suture marks is located in the left inguinal area. The penis is uncircumcised. No tattoos are noted. The distal phalanx of the right ring finger has been previously amputated and is well healed. Other distinctive external markings are absent.

DIAGNOSTIC AND THERAPEUTIC ARTIFACTS

An endotracheal tube exits from the right side of the mouth. Multiple perimortem needle puncture wounds are present in each subclavian region. A needle puncture mark with slight ecchymosis is located in the right cubital fossa. A small needle mark with underlying hematoma is present in the left radial fossa. EKG conductor pads are located over each breast and in the left lateral thoracic area.

POSTMORTEM CHANGES

Rigor mortis is generalized and well developed. Livor mortis is well developed, dorsal, the usual violet color, and blanches with light pressure. The eyes show early corneal clouding. The vermillion borders of the lips are slightly dry. Other postmortem changes are absent.

EXTERNAL EXAMINATION

The face is somewhat cyanotic and plethoric. The scalp and soft tissues of the face are otherwise normal. The nasal and facial bones are without palpable fracture. The conjunctival vessels are slightly congested and there are no ocular petechiae. A small amount of mucoid fluid is present in each nasal vestibule. The lips, gums, teeth, tongue, and buccal mucosa are normal and free of injury. The pinnae, external meati, and mastoid regions are normal.

The neck shows no indication of abrasion, contusion, or other abnormality except for moderate distension of neck veins. The neck is not excessively mobile.

The torso is free of injury and is symmetrical. No subcutaneous emphysema or cutaneous lesions are noted. The abdomen is moderately distended with gas.

The upper extremities are symmetrical, muscular, and well developed. No needle tracks or hesitation marks are present. A 0.5 cm resolving hematoma is present beneath the left thumbnail.

Two testes are palpable in the scrotum. The external genitalia, pudendum, and anorectal areas are normal except for a small external hemorrhoid at the two o'clock position.

The inguinal regions and buttocks are normal; no inguinal adenopathy is present. The lower extremities are symmetrical. There is slight hair loss in a sock-like distribution, and the toe nails are thickened and untrimmed.

In summary, external examination reveals no significant acute abnormalities and no acute injuries are noted other than diagnostic and therapeutic artifacts.

INTERNAL EXAMINATION

CHEST AND ABDOMEN

The skin of the chest and abdomen is reflected using the usual Y-shaped incision. Puncture of each hemithorax with a water filled syringe shows no indication of pneumothorax. Subcutaneous fat and musculature are normal and free of injury. The anterior chest wall and sternum are intact, and upon removal, there are no abnormal fluid collections in the chest or abdomen. No peculiar odors or color changes are identified. Examination of the organs in situ shows normal organ morphology and relationships. The viscera are congested. The diaphragm is normal.

The thoracic and abdominal organs are removed using the Virchow Technique, and are serially examined. The following notable findings are observed.

Cardiovascular System

The heart weighs 485 grams. The left ventricle demonstrates concentric hypertrophy with a left ventricular wall thickness of 2.1 cm. The coronary arteries are normally distributed and are widely patent throughout their lengths, with minimal, soft, atherosclerotic plaques focally. The epicardium, valve leaflets, chordae, and endocardium appear normal. The myocardium is reddish tan throughout and no focal myocardial lesions are observed. The thoracoabdominal aorta and major branches show moderate yellow, atherosclerotic streaking without ulceration. There are no vascular perforations.

Respiratory System

The trachea and bronchi are grossly normal except for a focal mucosal contusion adjacent to the endotracheal tube cuff, which is positioned appropriately. The hilar structures are normal. The major vessels are normally distributed and free of gross abnormalities. The lungs appear similar and have a combined weight of 960 grams. Each lung is congested and moderately edematous, exuding a pink-white foam on manual compression. No pneumonic changes are observed. There is no indication of thrombosis, embolism, infarction, or neoplasia. The apical visceral and parietal pleura are free of hemorrhage or perforating defects.

Gastrointestinal System

The serosa, wall, and mucosa of the esophagus, stomach, small bowel, colon, and rectum are grossly normal. The stomach contains approximately one cup of partially digested food, primarily consisting of green vegetable material.

Hepatobiliary System

The liver weighs 1650 grams and shows intense plum discoloration and congestion. There is no indication of fatty change or cirrhosis. No focal intrahepatic lesions are noted. The gallbladder contains about 15 cc of viscous green bile, no stones, and is grossly normal. The extrahepatic biliary ducts are patent. The pancreas shows the usual lobular architecture, mild autolysis, and is otherwise normal.

Urogenital System

The kidneys are symmetrical and have a combined weight of 320 grams. Each kidney shows congestion of the cortex and medulla. The capsule strips easily and the cortical surface is smooth. The cortico-medullary ratio is normal, as are the pyramids, calyces, and vessels. The ureters are of normal caliber. The urinary bladder is normal and contains approximately 100 cc of amber urine. The seminal vesicles are normal and the prostate is firm and nodular with slight enlargement.

Reticuloendothelial System

The spleen weighs 140 grams and is acutely congested. The capsule is tense and of normal thickness. The red and white pulp are normal. Nodes of the axillary, hilar, mediastinal, abdominal, and cervical area appear normal except to note mild anthracosis of the hilar nodes.

Musculoskeletal System

The axial skeleton is intact. Mild osteophytic lipping is noted on the thoraco-lumbar spine. Vertebral marrow space is grossly normal. Skeletal muscles are symmetrical and grossly normal in appearance.

Endocrine System

The thyroid gland is normal size, symmetrical, tan, and free of nodularity, hemorrhage, or cysts. The parathyroids are not identified grossly. The adrenals are of normal size and are free of nodularity or hemorrhage.

Neck

The skin of the neck is dissected up to the angle of the mandible. There is no evidence of soft tissue trauma to the major airways or vital structures in the lateral neck compartments. The hyoid bone and thyroid cartilages are free of fracture. The carotid vessels are pliable and patent. The epiglottis is not inflamed or swollen. There is no airway mucosal edema. No foreign objects are present in the airway, which contains moderate pulmonary edema foam. The anterior cervical spine and atlanto-occipital joint are intact.

Head

The scalp is reflected with the standard intermastoidal incision. There is no indication of scalp trauma. The calvarium is intact and shows moderate yellow discoloration.

The dura is intact and free of chronic discoloration or thickening. Diffuse subarachnoid hemorrhage is present over both convexities, and is most prominent at the base of the brain. Brain weight is 1540 grams. Slight, symmetrical uncal notching is noted, but there is no cerebellar tonsil herniation or cingulate shifting. No cortical contusions are seen. The Circle of Willis contains a 0.5 cm, ruptured berry aneurysm at the junction of the anterior communicating artery on the left. The cerebellum is normally formed. No focal or mass lesions are seen on the brain surface and the cortex is normal to palpation. Moderate cerebral edema is noted. The basilar skull and atlanto-occipital region are intact. See neuropathology report for further details on the brain.

REPORT OF HISTOLOGIC SECTIONS

A. Heart
B. Lung
C. Thyroid
D. Kidney
E. Liver/Spleen
F. Adrenal
G. Prostate
H. Berry aneurysm

Sections of heart, lung, thyroid, kidney, liver, spleen, adrenal, prostate, and berry aneurysm are examined. The aneurysm shows no inflammation or thrombosis, and adjacent brain shows subarachnoid hemorrhage. Cardiac sections show enlarged myocytes and nuclei.

Small and medium-sized vessels in the kidney and spleen show moderate arterial wall thickening. Other sections show nonspecific changes and are noncontributory, except for prostate which shows nodular stromal and glandular hyperplasia.

OTHER PROCEDURES

1. Vitreous for chemistries; electrolytes in normal range
2. Blood for ethanol concentration; negative
3. Urine for drug abuse screen; negative
4. Photos of berry aneurysm (gross and micro)
5. Intradepartmental consults: neuropathology
6. Retained tissues: berry aneurysm, routine stock
7. Special stains: none

FINAL ASSESSMENT

CLINICAL INFORMATION

1. Postcoital headache, coma, and death
2. Difficult, aborted attempts at central venous line placement

AUTOPSY FINDINGS

A. Anterior communicating cerebral artery, berry aneurysm
   - rupture of aneurysm with subarachnoid hemorrhage
   - cerebral edema
B. Myocardium, concentric left ventricular hypertrophy (mild to moderate)
C. Arterioles, hyaline arteriolosclerosis
D. Spinal column, osteoarthritis (mild)
E. Prostate, benign nodular hyperplasia
F. Anus, external hemorrhoid
G. Other findings:
   - Generalized visceral congestion
   - Pulmonary edema
   - No indication of thoracic injury

SUMMARY AND COMMENTS

Shorty after coitus, this 57-year-old black male complained of severe headache. He became unresponsive in the emergency room and was pronounced dead 47 minutes after arrival, approximately 75 minutes postcoital. Routine chemistries and blood count were within normal limits; other lab tests were not performed. Multiple unsuccessful attempts were made to place a subclavian line, causing clinical concern of possible thoracic or vascular injury.

Death is due to subarachnoid hemorrhage caused by a ruptured berry aneurysm. Rupture during stress and in the postcoital period are documented in the medical literature. Although hypertension had not been diagnosed clinically, cardiac hypertrophy and systemic arterial findings in this case are typical of hypertension, which also may predispose to rupture of berry aneurysms. There is no evidence of vasculitis. Subarachnoid hemorrhage has been associated with cocaine and other drug abuse, but blood alcohol and toxicologic drug screen were negative. Postmortem vitreous chemistries show normal electrolytes and renal function tests.

There is no indication of injury related to subclavian line insertion.

A recent review article concerning berry aneurysms is located in the September 1991 issue of *Speculative Medicine*, page 178.

Due to the sudden, unexpected nature of this death, the county medical examiner was notified of the death prior to autopsy at Anywhere County Hospital. The medical examiner declined to investigate or certify the death, but asked that they be notified if autopsy shows any evidence of injury or foul play.

For death certificate purposes, the cause of death could be listed as:

> Subarachnoid hemorrhage due to ruptured cerebral artery berry aneurysm.
> Other significant conditions: Probable hypertension.

- Investigative report
- Autopsy report
- Photographs and/or digital Images
- Police Report
- Copies of applicable medical records
- Reports of laboratory test results
- Evidence and property documentation
- Body receipt and release documentation

FIGURE 41.1   A typical death investigation file.

In addition to the autopsy report, a typical medical examiner or coroner case file will contain the types of information shown in Figure 41.1. Usually, the only information that the medical examiner or coroner would release from the file are those records and documentation prepared by the medical examiner's or coroner's office. Thus, police reports and medical records would not typically be released and copies would have to be obtained directly from those sources using established and required procedures. The medical examiner or coroner may also have other items, such as blocks of tissue used to prepare microscopic slides and the microscopic slides themselves. Also, but rarely, it is necessary to retain part or all of an organ as evidence or for further diagnostic study that cannot be completed before burial occurs. In such cases, the organ is usually held for a designated period of time and is then incinerated if not claimed by the next of kin.

42 A Day at the Medical Examiner's Office

The medical examiner's office described here is located in a major city having a population of about 500,000 people, and the office serves the entire county in which the city is located. About 5000 people die each year in the county (1% of the population), and approximately 2000 deaths (40% of all deaths) are reported to the office each year. Of the 2000 deaths reported to the office, about 500 are declined, and although a brief report is on file at the office, the medical examiner does not conduct a full investigation and does not sign the death certificate. The remaining 1500 cases usually consist of about 100 homicides, 100 suicides, 300 accidental deaths (of which about half are traffic accidents), a few cases in which the manner of death is undetermined, and the remaining 1000 or so cases involve natural deaths. Out of the 1500 cases fully investigated by the office, a scene investigation is conducted in about 700 cases, an autopsy is performed in about 700 cases, the body is examined only externally in about 350 cases, and the remaining 400 or so cases are signed out (certified) without examination of the body at the morgue. There are 3 medical examiners and a forensic fellow (pathologist) in training. Each medical examiner has to testify in a murder trial once or twice per month.

Each morning the medical examiner's staff meets. They review the death investigation reports completed by the investigators for deaths that occurred during the night and on the preceding evening. Decisions are made about what needs to be done on each case. A 10- to 15-minute educational session is held on an important topic. A few minutes are also spent discussing some challenging cases from the past and how they might be managed.

Today there are five cases to review. One involves an old man who was found dead in bed. After conducting an initial investigation, it was determined that the man had severe heart disease. His doctor was contacted and he agreed to sign the death certificate. This case went into the medical examiner's log book as a "declined jurisdiction case" because the medical examiner did not need to investigate the death. The other four cases involve a woman who was shot by her husband during a domestic argument, a man who had apparently committed suicide by sitting in his car while it was running in a closed garage, a young boy who ran out in front of a car, and a 25-year-old who dropped dead while playing basketball. The medical examiners decided that the two associates would each do one autopsy and the fellow would do two, thus taking care of the cases for the day. A medical student from the local medical school was also present to observe; she was spending a month at the office to see what forensic pathology was all about.

Soon after the autopsies were started, a call came into the office informing the investigator that a dead body had been found near some local railroad tracks. The fellow took off his gloves and gown, and traveled with the investigator to the death scene. After examining the body at the scene, it was discovered that the man had been shot in the head. Homicide detectives were called in and they processed the scene. The forensic fellow pronounced the man dead, and the body was transported to the medical examiner's office and placed in the cold storage area. Now there were five autopsies to be done that day. Because the fellow had already been assigned two cases, one of the associates would perform the autopsy on the man who was found near the railroad tracks.

The autopsies started at about 9:00 AM. By 2:00 PM the autopsies were completed. This medical examiner's office employs autopsy technicians who help with the examinations and removal of organs and cleanup, which speeds things up considerably. Also, having multiple technicians and pathologists allows more than one autopsy to be done at a time.

At 2:30 PM, the forensic fellow had a meeting with the district attorney about a case that was coming up for trial. One of the associates had a meeting with the homicide detectives to discuss the findings in the autopsy he did on the woman who was shot. The other associate had to go to the courthouse to testify in a trial that was taking place concerning a murder that happened about 8 months prior. At 3:00 PM, a reporter from the local television station showed up and interviewed the forensic fellow about the man found by the railroad tracks. The chief medical examiner was at the local medical school giving a lecture, and also had to speak to the Kiwanis Club at their noon luncheon. He also had an appointment with a family to discuss the findings of a death investigation he conducted about a week before.

Most of the rest of the day was spent dictating the findings from the autopsies so that typed reports could be prepared. Some time was also spent proofreading rough drafts from other reports. The forensic fellow was writing a scientific article stemming from a research project he was doing on the usefulness of some chemical tests on eye fluid to determine how long a person had been dead, and he spent some time on that project.

Right before the office closed, the staff got together again to discuss their cases and to make sure that no problems had arisen during the day. None had, and it was a fairly typical day as far as the medical examiner's office was concerned.

After the office closed, and after getting home, one of the associate medical examiner's beeper went off. It was the office calling. A man had just been run over by the subway train. He was off to the scene to meet the case investigator. Death doesn't stop at 5:00 PM. The scene investigation was conducted and the medical examiner got home at about 8:00 PM. The body was taken to the morgue and the autopsy was done the following morning, a Saturday. Death does not stop on weekends either.

The doctors and support staff who serve as medical examiners in this office really love their work. They work with police, attorneys, families, insurance companies, the media, public health agencies, and other people. They are not stuck in a hospital or doctor's office all day. Although they earn less money than many physicians or other professionals, they make a good living and they feel more than compensated by the important nature of their work and through their public service. They heartily recommend death investigation as a sound choice for a career. They know that regardless of technology and general job trends, there will always be a demand for their services because in the foreseeable future, deaths will continue to occur on a regular basis and people will want to know the cause and circumstances of death.

Further Reading

The Autopsy, Medicine, and Health Statistics (R. Hanzlick, Ed.), National Center for Health Statistics. DHHS Pub# 2001-1416. October 2001.

College of American Pathologists, *Basic Competencies in Forensic Pathology: A Forensic Pathology Primer* (Joseph Prahlow, Ed.). Northfield, IL, 2006.

College of American Pathologists, *Cause of Death and the Death Certificate* (R. Hanzlick, Ed.). Northfield, IL, (in press).

Hanzlick, R., Coroner training needs: a numeric and geographic analysis. *JAMA*, 276, 1775–1778, 1996.

Hanzlick, R., The conversion of coroner systems to medical examiners in the US: a lull in the action. *Am. J. Forensic Med. Pathol.* (in press).

Hanzlick, R., Medical examiners, coroners, and public health: a review and update. *Arch. Pathol. Lab. Med.* (in press).

Hanzlick, R., Combs, D., Parrish, R.G., and Ing, R.T. Death investigation in the United States, 1990: a survey of statutes, systems, and education requirements. *J. Forensic Sciences*, 39, 628–632, 1993.

Hanzlick, R. and Combs, D. Medical examiner and coroner systems: history and trends. *JAMA*, 279, 870–874, 1998.

Hanzlick, R. and Graham, M. *Forensic Pathology in Criminal Cases*, 2nd ed. Lexis-Nexis Publishing, Albany, NY, 2001. (405 pages plus appendices, 3rd edition in press.)

Hanzlick, R. and Parrish, R.G., Epidemiologic aspects of forensic pathology. *Clinics in Laboratory Medicine*, 18, 23–37, 1998.

Hanzlick, R. and Parrish, R.G., The use of medical examiner/coroner data in public health surveillance and epidemiologic research. *Annual Review of Public Health*, 17, 383–409, 1996.

Institute of Medicine, *Medicolegal Death Investigation System: Workshop Summary*. The National Academies Press. Washington, DC, 2003.

National Association of Medical Examiners, *A Guide for Manner of Death Classification*. Atlanta, Georgia. Available at http://www.TheNAME.org.

Randall, B., *Death Investigation: The Basics*. Galen Press, Tucson, AZ, 1997.

Spitz, W., *Spitz and Fisher's Medicolegal Investigation of Death: Guidelines for the Application of Pathology to Crime Investigation*, 4th ed. Charles C. Thomas, Springfield, IL, 2006.

Useful Web Sites

Accreditation Council for Graduate Medical Education
www.acgme.org

American Academy of Forensic Sciences
www.aafs.org

American Board of Medicolegal Death Investigators
www.slu.edu/organizations/abmdi/

American Board of Pathology
www.abpath.org

Centers for Disease Control and Prevention Death Investigation Information
www.cdc.gov/epo/dphsi/mecisp/index.htm

College of American Pathologists
www.cap.org

International Association of Coroners and Medical Examiners
www.theiacme.com/

National Association of Medical Examiners
www.TheNAME.org

National Center for Health Statistics
www.cdc.gov/nchs

For many other links and related information see:

COMECA (Coordinating Office for Medical Examiner/Coroner Activities)
www.fcmeo.org/COMECA.htm

NODIA (Network on Death Investigation Affairs)
Click on NODIA on menu bar on the NAME website at www.TheNAME.org

Index

A

Accident, 57, 113, 131
Administrative remedy, 129
Alabama, 89
Alaska, 89
Alzheimer's disease, 60
American Academy of Forensic Sciences
    (AAFS), 137–138
American Board of Medicolegal Death
    Investigators (ABMDI), 45, 138
American Board of Pathology (ABP), 18, 138
American Society of Clinical Pathology (ASCP),
    138
Ancillary investigation, 8–9
Arizona, 89
Arkansas, 89
Armed Forces medical examiner, 103
Assistant coroner, 46
Autopsy, 8
    authorization, 63
    cost, 29, 65
    educational conference following, 65
    etymology, 8
    evaluation of medical care and, 66
    findings, 4, 15, 110
        interpretation of, 71
        use of, 71
    full, 8
    in institute-based death investigation, 23, 59,
        66
    legislation, 21
    permission, 107–108
    in private death investigation, 12, 14, 59
    report, 9
        completion of, 65
        copies of, 68
        for hospital-based death investigation, 66
        information in, 109–111
            cause, manner, and circumstances of
                death, 111
            comment or opinion, 111
            date, time, and place of examination
                as well as attendees, 109
            diagnostic and therapeutic artifacts,
                109–110
            external examination of body, 110

features of identification, 110
final diagnoses and findings, 110–111
internal examination of body, 110
postmortem changes, 109
postmortem imaging studies, 109
preliminary findings, 110
presentation, clothing. personal effects
    and evidence, 109
reason for performing examination,
    109
test results, 110
for institution-based death investigation,
    66
preparation of, 9
questions in, 67
sample of, 149–155
restricted, 8
venue, 25–26
work station, 27

B

Ballistics, 49, 51
Botany, 49, 51
Bureau of Alcohol, Tobacco, and Firearms, 101
Bureau of Indian Affairs, 103

C

California, 90
Case record, 9
Chain of custody, 123
Chief medical investigator, 42
Civil law, 147
Clinical-pathologic correlation, 67
Cocaine, 133
College of American Pathologists (CAP), 65, 138
Colorado, 90
Connecticut, 90
Coroner(s), 7, 18–19
    assistant, 46
    complaints about, 37
    deputy, 46
    etymology, 35
    historical perspectives, 35–36
    medical examiners *vs.*, 43

pathologist, 19
political ties, 36
position requirements, 36
role, 4, 37
state laws, 37
Cremains, 122
Crime lab report, 58
Crime laboratory, 25
Criminal law, 147
Criminalistics, 49, 50

D

D-MAT team, 101
D-MORT team, 101
Death
accidental, 57
classification, 135
cocaine-related, 133
from complications of medical procedures, 133
drug-related, 133
of federal property, 103
from forced police shootings, 133
homicidal, 57
on Indian reservations, 103
manner of, 57
natural, 57
of prison inmates, 145
pronouncement, 143–143
official *vs.* actual data, 143
reportable, 85–86
suicidal, 57
types investigated, 86
undetermined, 57
while in police custody, 145
Death certificate, 58
as opinions of certifier, 115
preliminary, 65
purpose of
clarification of cause and circumstances of death, 113
documentation of fact of death, 113
information about deceased, 113
information about disposition of remains, 113
U.S. standard, 116
Death investigation(s)
access to information resulting from, 141–142
classic dilemmas, 133–135
disagreement with outcome, 129–130
disciplines associated with
ballistics, 49
botany, 49

criminalistics, 49
engineering, 49
entomology, 49
firearms analysts, 49
jurisprudence, 49
latent prints, 49
nursing, 49, 52
odontology, 49
pathology, 49
physical anthropology, 49
psychiatry and behavioral science, 49
questioned documents, 49
radiology, 49
toxicology, 49
funding, 29
funeral arrangements and, 121–122
hospital-based, 65–67
cost, 12
laboratory tests for, 81
review of medical records in, 65
institution-based, 11, 14, 18, 27
autopsy, 121
permission for, 107
report, 109
autopsy in, 23, 59, 66
example of, 63–68
funding, 29
goals of, 59–60
location, 27
rake analogy and, 81
insurance policies and, 131–132
laboratory tests in, 8, 17, 58, 81
medicolegal, 11, 21–23, 57–58
autopsy report, 109
examples of, 87–88
funding of, 29
goals of, 58
location of, 27
rake analogy and, 81
systems for, 87–88
types, 19
by state, 89–98
typical, 73–78
person responsible for conducting, 17–20
private, 12, 14, 17, 23, 66
in Alzheimer's disease, 60
autopsy in, 12, 14, 59, 108
example of, 69–71
funding, 29
goals of, 59–60
typical, 69–71
unique aspects of, 70
venue, 27
professional organizations, 137–139
public health, 13–15

reason for, 3–5
    evaluation of transplant donors, 4
    institutional concerns, 3
    legal, 3
    medical care quality, 3
    personal, 3–4
    public health and safety, 3
    research, 4
    taxpayer funding, 4–5
resolution of questions and controversies, 129
retrospective, 13
series, 13
specimen analysis, 81
state laws, 21
steps, 7–8
    examination of body, 7–8
    initial collection of information, 7
    scene investigation, 7
types of, 11–12
venue, 25
Death investigator(s), 45–46, 73
    major functions, 74–75
    professional organizations, 137–139
Delaware, 90–91
Department of Homeland Security, 102
Deputy coroner, 46
Disaster medical assistance team, 101
Disaster mortuary operations and recovery team,
    101
Disaster plan, 101
Disinterment, 119
District of Columbia, 91
Double indemnity clause, 131

E

Embalming, 122
Engineering, 49, 50–51
Entomology, 49, 51
Epidemiological research, 13
    incidence, 13
    prevalence, 13
    risk factors, 13
Evidence
    analysis, 123
    classic characteristics, 124–125
    obtainment, 123
    preservation, 123
    principles, 123–125
    recognition, 123
    steps in processing, 124
    transmission, 123
    unique characteristics, 125

Exhumation, 119–120
    defined, 119
Expert
    defined, 127–128
    professionally recognized, 127
Expert witness, 128
External causes, 113

F

Fact witness, 127, 128
Federal Bureau of Investigation (FBI), 102
Final report, 9
Firearm examiners, 49, 51
Florida, 92
Forensic nursing, 52
Forensic science lab, 25
Forensic scientists, 25, 49–54, 80

G

Georgia, 41, 88, 92
Gross findings, 65

H

Hawaii, 92
Homicide, 57, 113
Hospital-based death investigation(s), 65–67. *See
    also* Institution-based
    investigation(s)
    cost, 12
    laboratory tests for, 81
    review of medical records in, 65

I

Idaho, 92
Illinois, 93
Indian reservations, 103
Indiana, 93
Institution-based death investigation(s), 11, 14,
    18, 27
    autopsy, 121
        permission for, 107
        report, 109
    example of, 63–68
    funding, 29
    goals of, 59–60
    location, 27
    rake analogy and, 81
Insurance policies, 131–132

International Association of Coroners and
    Medical Examiners (IACME), 138
Investigative report, 58, 66–67, 78

J

Jurisprudence, 49, 52

K

Kansas, 19, 93
Kentucky, 93

L

Laboratory tests, 8, 17, 58, 81
Latent prints, 49, 50
Legislation
    postmortem examination, 21
    state anatomy, 21
    state autopsy, 21
    state death investigation, 21
Louisiana, 19, 93

M

Macroscopic findings, 65
Maine, 93
Manner of death, 57
Maryland, 20, 93
Mass disaster, 27
Mass fatality incidents, 101–102
Massachusetts, 93–94
Medical examiner(s), 7, 41–43
    birth of, 42
    coroners vs., 43
    defined, 19
    historical perspectives, 42
    office, 157–159
    overall role, 4
Medical procedures, 133
Medicolegal death investigation(s), 11, 21–23,
    57–58
    autopsy report, 109
    examples of, 87–88
    funding, 29
    goals of, 58
    location, 27
    rake analogy and, 81
    systems for, 87–88
    types, 19
        by state, 89–98
    typical, 73–78

Michigan, 20, 41, 94
Minnesota, 94
Mississippi, 94
Missouri, 94
Model Postmortem Examinations Act (1954), 21,
    85
Montana, 94
Morgue, temporary facilities, 27
Murder, etymology, 35

N

National Association of Medical Examiners
    (NAME), 135, 137
National Transportation Safety Board (NTSB),
    101
Natural death, 57
Nebraska, 94
Nevada, 94–95
New Hampshire, 95
New Jersey, 88, 95
New Mexico, 20, 42, 88, 95
New York, 95
North Carolina, 20, 41, 95
North Dakota, 19, 95

O

Odontology, 49, 51–52
Ohio, 19, 87–88, 95–96
Oklahoma, 96
Open record law, 141
Oregon, 96

P

Pathogenesis, 17
Pathologist, 7
    board certified, 18, 138
    board qualified, 18, 138
    defined, 17
    educational background, 18
    forensic, 33–34
Pathology, 49, 52
    anatomic, 17
    clinical, 17
    forensic, 17
Pennsylvania, 96
Per capita costs, 29
Physical anthropology, 51
Police custody, 145
Police laboratory, 25
Police report, 58

Police shootings, forced, 133
Preliminary death certificate, 65
Prison inmates, 145
Private death investigation(s), 12, 14, 17, 23, 66
   in Alzheimer's disease, 60
   autopsy in, 12, 14, 59, 108
   example of, 69–71
   funding, 29
   goals of, 59–60
   typical, 69–71
   unique aspects of, 70
   venue, 27
Psychiatry and behavioral science, 49, 52
Public health death investigations, 13–15

Q

Questioned documents, 49, 50

R

Radiology, 49, 52
Rake analogy, 79–81
Rhode Island, 96

S

Scene investigation, 7
Serology and forensic biology, 51
South Carolina, 96
South Dakota, 96
Specimen analysis, 81
Stock tissue, 65

Suicide, 57, 113
Suicide exclusion clause, 131
Sunshine law, 141
Surveillance, 13

T

Temporary morgue facilities, 27
Tennessee, 96
Texas, 96–97
Tort, 58
Toxicology, 49–50

U

Undetermined death, 57
Utah, 97

V

Vermont, 41, 97
Virginia, 97

W

Washington, 97
West Virginia, 41, 97
Wheel analogy, 80
Wisconsin, 41, 97
Witnesses, 128
Wyoming, 97